"James Eby has done every committed Christian a great service by writing *World Impacting Churches*. This book is a passionate call to the entire Church with clear guidelines that could launch a new, invigorated global movement for the cause of Jesus Christ in our time."

-Dr. David Shibley,
President, Global Advance

"James Eby is a global leader in missions who practices exactly what he preaches. This book comes from a life spent in pursuit of God and totally focused on finishing Jesus' commandment to take the gospel to every person. James Eby has trained and mobilized thousands and is well qualified to share his experience in Christian missions. His book will inspire and equip you for that task."

-Iain Muir,
International Director, Youth With A Mission

"No other book I know of presents the overarching challenge of the unfinished task so concisely, so comprehensively and so readably. Here is something you can trust and use and recommend. Superb job!"

-Ralph D. Winter,
Founder, U. S. Center for World Mission

"James Eby's passion, knowledge, and experience come through in this challenging book. Years of international ministry are made practical for individuals and congregations as Eby opens his heart. This is a must read for any person or pastor desiring to learn more about how to fulfill the Great Commission!"

-Dr. A. D. Beacham, Jr.,
Executive Director, World Missions Ministries,
International Pentecostal Holiness Church

"Reading *World Impacting Churches* by James Eby is a profound spiritual experience. I urge everyone that has a heart for God and for a lost, hurting world to receive the message of this wonderful book with an open and tender heart. *World Impacting Churches* is a God-given task that can be done by this generation. Please let the reading of James Eby's new book be a priority. You will be blessed and motivated by this powerful message."

-Dr. Syvelle Phillips,
Founder/President, Evangel Bible Translators

"Though reared in a small Eastern Oklahoma town, God birthed a global vision in James Eby's heart. Referred to by a college president as 'the most analytical student I ever taught,' Jim demonstrates this trait in *World Impacting Churches*. However, as you read this book, you also catch the passion of his heart for God and his vision for reaching the world's unreached millions. Is it possible to fulfill the Great Commission in this generation and to impact the world in the process? Do we need a new missions mindset and a revolutionary approach to global evangelization? Does that approach include effectively training national leaders? Jim's book answers a resounding 'yes' to all the above questions. Though written primarily to help train a new generation of church planters in the 10/40 Window, Jim's '10 Essential Characteristics for Changing the World and Finishing The Great Commission' are applicable to any church in any country which desires to participate in the global harvest. The insights contained in this book enable each of us to personally join the effort to finish Christ's assignment in this generation. I highly recommend this book to all who share Jim's passion that reaching people for Christ is not just our 'duty' but our greatest privilege and joy. Thanks Jim for applying your principles and passion and leading me to Jesus Christ."

-Dr. Bob R. Ely,
President, Southwestern Christian University

"James Eby's teaching is making a significant impact on our national church planting movement in Cambodia and is helping to touch our entire nation for Christ. His teaching is passionate, powerful, practical and effective. Without reservation, I recommend this excellent book *World Impacting Churches* to all pastors and ministry leaders everywhere who desire to be more effective for Christ."

-Rev. Barnabas Mam,
National Director, Ambassadors for Christ Cambodia; Founder, Institute of Church Planting Cambodia; Senior Minister, Living Hope in Christ Church

"James Eby writes *World Impacting Churches* with a sense of deep commitment and passion and broad experience as a seasoned missionary. His theme is one of the most vital of our day. God's heart is to use the entire Body of Christ to finish the Great Commission in our generation. The signs of the times are around us. We are living in the midst of Matthew 24 and Luke 21. The impact of reading this book should incite all readers to organize their lives and resources around obeying the Great Commandment and completing the Great Commission."

-Dr. Howard Foltz,
Professor of Global Evangelization, Regent University; Founder and CEO, AIMS

"Whenever you combine passion with practical application, the end result can be powerful. *World Impacting Churches* is a powerful book that passionately encourages the Church to respond to the task Jesus gave us and provides practical ideas as to how this directive can be accomplished. As Jim's pastor, I can attest to the fact that he is living his life for world evangelism and his life adds great weight to his words."

-Alan Clayton,
*Senior Pastor, The Ark Family Church,
Conroe, Texas*

"I have had the privilege of knowing Pastor James Eby for some time and personally witnessing his passion for completing the Great Commission in this generation. He loves India and is truly an Indian in his heart. Pastor Eby is being tremendously used by the Lord to mobilize the Body of Christ to reach the whole of India through his powerful Great Commission Conferences being held across the nation. His book *World Impacting Churches* is powerful and practical, full of clear thought and strategies which can be reproduced in every culture and society. I am certain this book will impact thousands of readers in India and around the world and instill an unquenchable passion to see the task finished in our lifetime. I strongly recommend this book as one of the best training manuals on the Great Commission I have seen. It should be taught to every believer in every church, Bible school, and training institute. If we practice the contents of this book, we will soon see the Great Commission finished. May the Lord multiply the fruit of this book in the hands of our loving Master who fed the multitudes."

-Dr. Alex Abraham,
Operation Agape—a pioneer church planting movement in North India

"James Eby's book will awaken today's Christians for World Missions and motivate church and missions leaders to develop and sharpen strategies for their local churches to finish the work of missions in this generation. This is not just a book. This is the embodiment of Jim's life. He has a great passion for World Missions which comes from his deep compassion for souls. Jim is a strategist who has practiced and shown these ways in his daily life. I met him 26 years ago in London as one of his students, and from then until now I have seen his integrity and consistency in living up to his role as a vanguard of World Missions. It is my great privilege and delight to use this book as a text, not only for our church's mission department, but also for our PGM missionary training school."

-Rev. Sung Kee Ho,
Senior Pastor, Antioch Church of Philadelphia
(Presbyterian); President, Professionals for
Global Missions

"This book is timely, inspiring, and challenging. It is an invaluable manual for every church leader who truly and earnestly desires to make a meaningful impact in the area of church planting in this generation."

-Rev. Francis Olubambi,
President, Vision International Christian Ministries
(VICM), Lagos, Nigeria

"In a day of globalization, God's people everywhere are being called to share the good news with all peoples. No longer is mission emanating only from the West; in fact, non-Western churches are leading the way in mission to the ends of the earth. Jim's work encourages every congregation of believers everywhere to participate faithfully in seeing that God's name is known and worshipped by all peoples. May God use this book for the glory of His name."

-Dr. Elaine Vaden,
Associate Director,
Presbyterian Frontier Fellowship

"If there was ever a time to mobilize the Church for the Great Commission it is now. The Church must become burdened with a sense of urgency for finishing the assignment Jesus gave us. The message conveyed in *World Impacting Churches* should be taken to every church as an exhortation to people who believe and follow Christ to step out, press on, and complete the task."

-Mohan Philip,
Uttar Pradesh Mission, North India

WORLD IMPACTING CHURCHES

WORLD IMPACTING CHURCHES

---

10 Essential Characteristics for Changing the World
& Finishing The Great Commission

JAMES R. EBY

TATE PUBLISHING *& Enterprises*

Published by Tate Publishing & Enterprises, LLC
127 E. Trade Center Terrace | Mustang, Oklahoma 73064 USA
1.888.361.9473 | www.tatepublishing.com

Tate Publishing is committed to excellence in the publishing industry. The company reflects the philosophy established by the founders, based on Psalms 68:11,
"The Lord gave the word and great was the company of those who published it."

Book design copyright © 2007 by Tate Publishing, LLC. All rights reserved.
Cover design by Rusty Eldred
Interior design by Elizabeth A. Mason

Published in the United States of America

ISBN:978-1-6024735-3-9
07.05.21

To Peggy, my beautiful wife, my one true love, my best friend, and my faithful companion for 41 years.

and

To my brothers and sisters in the Two-Thirds World who constantly inspire me with their commitment, who continually amaze me with their faith and vision, who are now taking the leading role in finishing *The Great Commission,* and who are impacting the world in the process.

Acknowledgements and Gratitude:

- To Peggy for her patience, her encouragement, and her first-class editorial comments.

- To my daughter, Dr. Ellen Moore, and to my life-long friend, Edith Ely, for their excellent editorial notes.

- To my family, Phillip and Ellen Moore, David and Andrea Eby, and Jonathan and LaNita Eby for their loving support and encouragement in the writing of this book and in the ministry of Mission Catalyst International.

- To my eight wonderful grandchildren (Jon Rush, Joshua, Meagan, Madison, Atticus, Aidan, Mac, and Sadie Beth) who love to hear Papa's stories and see the pictures from his travels around the world.

- To Dr. Harold Kurtz, for his guidance during the early formation of this book.

- To those committed missionaries who blazed the trail before me and who also had a passion to help finish *The Great Commission.*

- To all of the authors, lecturers, teachers, and speakers who have poured into my life for the past forty years and without whose input this book would not be possible. I am certain that many of the thoughts and ideas expressed herein should be attributed to them and would be if my memory would serve me better.

"In view of the constraining memories of the Cross of Christ and the love wherewith He hath loved us, let us rise and resolve, at whatever the cost of self-denial, that, live or die, we shall live or die for the evangelization of the world in our day."

...Missionary Statesman John R. Mott

CONTENTS

AUTHOR'S NOTES

Following are a number of notes with which you should become familiar before diving into this book. Thank you for your patience in reading these.

Throughout the book I will use the terms *Great Commission Churches* and *Impact Churches* as synonyms. I find these terms helpful in describing churches which have ten basic characteristics through which they tend to powerfully impact the world around them and help to finish *The Great Commission*.

You will find that I use the terms "Two-Thirds World" and "Majority World" synonymously to describe the countries that make up Asia, Africa, and Latin America which are economically developing at the moment. Both of these terms are, in my opinion, more respectful than the terms *Third World* or *Developing World* which are often used to describe these countries which together contain two-thirds of the population of the entire planet. Several of these countries are already beginning to take the lead role in the work of world missions and deserve our respect. As they are learning from the West, there are also many things we can learn from them.

You will note that the term *The Great Commission* is italicized throughout the text. I emphasize *The Great*

Commission as a divine mandate from Christ to His Body. It was His final directive to us before ascending to be with the Father and deserves our most profound respect and obedience.

This book has much to say about *Unreached Peoples* in relation to finishing *The Great Commission.* I understand there is considerable discussion and debate over what constitutes a people group, how many there are, how many are still unreached by the Gospel, and a host of other important questions. This can get a bit complicated. For this book I have chosen to use the figures as reported by *Joshua Project,* a ministry of the U. S. Center for World Mission which operates out of Colorado Springs, Colorado (USA). According to *Joshua Project,* at the time of this writing there are 9,605 different ethnic groups in the world. When each group is counted separately in each country of residence, it makes a total of 15,899 people groups in the world. Many of these groups develop different dialects and some different cultural traits in the various countries in which they live.

Of these 15,899 people groups, 9,482 are categorized as *reached* people groups and 6,417 are considered *unreached* with the Gospel. Of the world's 6,417 *Unreached Peoples,* 3,381 of them (53%) are small groups with less than 10,000 in total population (or population unknown). When checking these figures with *Joshua Project* (or any other credible source), please keep in mind that these figures change regularly as new information is gained.

I am indebted to people and organizations such as Dr. Ralph Winter and his *U.S. Center for World*

Mission, together with the *Perspectives* course, *Joshua Project,* the *International Mission Board* of the Southern Baptist Convention, Dr. Howard Foltz and his "Harvest Connection" teaching, Patrick Johnstone and his book *Operation World,* David Barrett with his *World Christian Encyclopedia,* Jim Montgomery and the *DAWN* movement, and many others for the significant work they have done in the areas of world evangelization and targeting *Unreached Peoples.* Most of the information in this book is because of their efforts.

This is a book which speaks much about finishing *The Great Commission* in this generation. While it must be admitted from the outset that it is very difficult, if not impossible, to know exactly how and when *The Great Commission* will be fulfilled, this must not deter us from our passion to see the Lord's mandate completed. Our objective must be to see a *Church Planting Movement* take place among each people group on earth. As this happens, *The Great Commission* can and will be completed.

You will read much about the 10/40 *Window* on the following pages. The 10/40 *Window* is an imaginary rectangle whose bottom line is 10 degrees latitude north of the Equator and whose top line is 40 degrees latitude north. Essentially the area covers North Africa, the Middle East, most of central, southern, and southeastern Asia and Japan. The 10/40 *Window* is so important because the vast majority of the world's *Unreached Peoples* live in this part of the world and yet only about three percent of the world's missionary work force is currently laboring there. If we are to finish the work of *The Great Commission,* we must concentrate on this part of the world for prayer and missionary church planting.

The use of the term *church* in this book has almost nothing to do with church buildings. It has only to do with congregations of God's people in a given locality, whether or not they have a church building and regardless of the form or size they take. The Church of Jesus Christ is not composed of brick and mortar; it is made up of people, and the form, size, and method of operation of individual congregations are many and varied.

It should be noted that many church planting organizations throughout the 10/40 *Window* are following one of the models of the New Testament and are having enormous success by focusing on planting *house churches* rather than larger congregations which require expensive buildings and full-time paid workers. This is contributing significantly to the finishing of *The Great Commission* and will be discussed in detail in Chapter 15.

As we talk about the critical need for planting "indigenous churches," it should be noted that anything which is truly indigenous will seem strange to the missionary working among the people group. If the work does not feel strange or awkward to the missionary, it likely is not genuinely indigenous. Because works which are truly indigenous do feel so odd, most missionaries do not plant indigenous churches. Rather they plant churches which have a hint of being native but which, in the end, feel somewhat comfortable to the missionaries. For a better understanding of this subject, please read *Searching for the Indigenous Church* by

Gene Daniels (William Carey Library, Pasadena, CA, USA, 2005).

Throughout the book I will often use the pronoun *he* or *him* in referring to pastors or other leaders. I am using these pronouns in the generic sense and intend to include women as well as men in all of these references. Many outstanding women are being used by God around the world in nearly every leadership capacity of the Church. If we are to indeed finish *The Great Commission* in this generation, we cannot do so with one-half of our army on the sidelines. We must have the help of the women of the world—especially those who have leadership giftings and callings. These women must be released to fulfill their God-given destinies in the world.

In the book I speak much about God's "Kingdom." Because the Kingdom has to do with God's rule in the earth and because its liberating message is such good news to people, I have chosen to capitalize "Kingdom." It should be noted that the expressions "kingdom of God" as used by Luke and "kingdom of heaven" as used by Matthew are, for all intents and purposes, interchangeable. They mean essentially the same thing in my opinion. The difference in the terms has to do primarily with the audiences which the writers were addressing.

In speaking of the role of workers in the Kingdom, I hesitate to use the term *laymen* because the New Testament record fails to distinguish between a professional *clergy* and the rest of God's people. I do so, however, because most of the world has bought into this false dichotomy. In the Scriptures, distinction between believers is not on the basis of whether they are professionally trained or not but rather on the basis of giftings and callings. Many *laymen* (as we use the term) in the New Testament were powerfully used by God and are vital keys today for reaching the world for Christ.

The term "Evangelicals" is used throughout the book in the broad sense and includes the Pentecostals, charismatics, and independents.

INTRODUCTION

"If you love me, you will obey what I command."

(John 14:15, NIV)

Two thousand years should be long enough to have an assignment from Jesus without finishing it! It is almost unimaginable that, even though the *final* instruction from our Lord was, "Go therefore and make disciples of all the nations..." (Matthew 28:19), still we have not come close to completing the mandate. Although Jesus' followers have made significant strides toward fulfilling *The Great Commission*, there remain more than 6,000 ethnic groups in the world who are officially categorized as *Unreached Peoples.*

Twenty centuries have now passed since Jesus' command was given, and yet more than one-fourth of the world's population has yet to hear an understandable presentation of the Gospel for the first time. Approximately 39% of people alive today belong to an ethnic group without a viable church among them.[1] Nearly every time a heart beats, someone dies somewhere in the world who has never heard of Jesus' love and power to save. Unbelievable! Surely the Church of

Jesus Christ can do better than that! Surely our love for Jesus and our obedience to His final command is more fervent and lasting than we have shown. Surely our ability to plan and work strategically is greater than we have demonstrated. Surely we can impact the world more profoundly than we have done.

The primary focus of this book is to help God's people throughout the earth gain new vision, more passion, greater determination, and clearer strategy for finishing *The Great Commission* in this generation—and to powerfully impact the world around them in the process. I am well aware that Christians in other generations also called for the finishing of *The Great Commission* and that they labored diligently to see it happen. Although significant progress has been made in many countries of the world and among many people groups, obviously the assignment has not been completed. I do believe, however, that Dr. C. Peter Wagner is correct when he says that, *for the first time in history* Jesus' followers now have a realistic opportunity to finish *The Great Commission* (italics mine). I am convinced it can be done in this generation. A number of achievements have been made during the past century which cause things to be different now and which provide an unusual opportunity to see Jesus' vision for the world completed. Several of those issues will be discussed at the conclusion of this writing. First, it is high time to see how this *realistic opportunity* to complete *The Great Commission,* of which Wagner speaks, can become a certainty. In order for it to happen, Jesus' commission must become our obsession. When I say *our* obsession, I am talking about the Body of Christ around the world. Each one will have to do his part. Thousands and thousands of individuals, churches, ministries, and organizations across the earth must catch fire with this vision to complete *The Great Commission* and unite our hearts, our prayers, our strategies, our efforts, and our resources in order to see it happen.

As was stated in the "Author's Notes," it must be admitted that it is difficult, if not impossible, to know exactly how and when *The Great Commission* will be fulfilled. However, this must not deter us from our passion to see the Lord's mandate fulfilled. Our objective must be a *Church Planting Movement* among each people group on earth. As this happens, *The Great Commission* can and will be completed.

As God's people prepared to move into the twenty-first century, more than 500 strategists for global evangelization assembled at the *Amsterdam 2000* conference to discuss the question, "What must we do in the coming decade to complete the task of world evangelization?" Among the wise and essential objectives set by the conference participants were the following:[2]

- To work toward the planting of churches within every remaining people group as we seek to evangelize and make disciples;

- To accelerate the multiplication of church planting movements in the 10/40 Window and other needy areas;

- To continue to mobilize significant, strategic focused prayer for the unfinished task and to raise up workers for the harvest;

- To work together more intentionally and inclusively, through alliances, networks, and partnerships—sharing contacts, information and resources (We do this to demonstrate unity with one another as evidence of the deity of Christ and his love for the world);

- To empower and provide training in evangelism, discipleship and church planting for younger leaders as well as laypeople;

- To encourage extensive and innovative initiatives to reach and disciple children and young people in each new generation;

- To allocate a much larger portion of our resources toward the least-reached areas of the world;

- To seek to use media, technology and other creative means more effectively to spread the gospel among the masses;

- To stay personally involved in grassroots evangelism so that our presentation of the biblical gospel is relevant, contextualized and meaningful;

- To live out the gospel as we seek to meet the physical and social needs of those to whom we minister with practical expressions of love and compassion.

- To assist in the work of scripture translation and distribution, recognizing its necessity as a foundation for all evangelism and church growth; and

- To ensure that all of our strategic plans of evangelism are biblically based and guided by the fourfold scope of Acts 1:8 (Jerusalem, Judea, Samaria, and the uttermost parts of the earth).

It is in response to and in harmony with this call, that this book is written. May God grant that the assignment Jesus gave us with His departing words will indeed be completed in this generation, and may He use this volume in some way to enhance the effort. Along with many other of God's people around the world, I share the dream that the Church of Jesus Christ will arise with new vision and passion to see Jesus' Kingdom come so that the Gospel will be preached to the poor, freedom will be proclaimed to prisoners, the blind will recover their sight, the oppressed will be released, and the Lord's favor will be proclaimed (Luke 4:18–19). As this happens, the world will indeed be impacted and we will help to usher in the return of Jesus Christ to the earth as King of Kings and Lord of Lords—and to see His Kingdom come in its fullness (Matthew 24:14).

ENDNOTES

1   *Missions Frontiers* magazine.   May-June, 2006 Issue, U. S. Center for World Mission.   Pasadena, CA, pp 8-9.

2   February, 2006 issue of Lausanne World Pulse.com: Article entitled *"World Evangelization Analysis – Strategy Working Group"* by Paul Eshleman.

GOD'S VISION FOR THE WORLD

"...and that repentance and remission of sins should be preached in His name to all *nations,* beginning at Jerusalem."

(Luke 24:47, italics added)

While banished to the Isle of Patmos for the Word of God and the testimony of Jesus Christ, the apostle John received a glimpse of God's vision for the world—a dream which had been in His heart for ages and generations. In the vision John was enabled to see prophetically into eternity. Before him and around the throne of God was an extremely large and diverse group of worshiping people. This is how John described the scene: "After these things I looked, and behold, a great multitude which no one could number, of all nations, tribes, peoples, and tongues, standing before the throne and before the Lamb, clothed with white robes, with palm branches in their hands..." (Revelation 7:9).

This revelation of God's desire not only captured John's imagination, it should capture ours as well. For in this vision God showed us both His longing and His plan for humanity. God's vision is to have major representation from each of the 16,000 ethnic groups in the world with Him in Heaven—people from every tribe, nationality, and language group on the face of the earth worshiping Him and giving Him the glory He so rightly deserves. This goal is also shown in the words of Jesus in Matthew 24:14: "And this gospel of the kingdom will be preached in the whole world as a testimony to all *nations,* and then the end will come." You will note that I have italicized the word *nations.* In the New Testament, the word translated *nations* does not normally refer to geopolitical nations such as India, China, Ecuador, or Kenya. In the Greek, the word is *ethne* (ethnic groups). The rendition of *ethne* as *nations* in many of the translations of the Bible is somewhat unfortunate in that it tends to give us a distorted perspective of the assignment which Jesus actually gave us. Jesus' clear command was not for us to make disciples in the individual countries of the world, but rather to make disciples of *each* of the world's ethnic groups.

The same understanding is true in the Old Testament. In those days people did not normally think of *nations* as we have come to understand them today. Their thinking was more along the line of *people groups.* The *nations* so often referred to in the Old Testament text were normally groups of ethno-linguistic peoples who occupied a certain territory. The grouping of *geopolitical* nations, as we have come to know them, is a rather new concept historically.

God's Kingdom—a Multi-ethnic Group of People

It is clear from these verses, along with numerous other passages of Scripture, that God's vision is for His Kingdom to be comprised of a multi-ethnic group of people which encompasses the entirety of His creation. For many years much of the Body of Christ appears to have missed this intention of God. At least it seems not to have been in clear focus in many of our missionary endeavors. As we have "gone into all the world," our evangelism objectives have often focused on the geopolitical nations rather than on the many people groups within each country. Ralph Winter reminds us, for example, that although Nigeria appears to be one country, it is in reality comprised of 427 ethno-linguistic peoples. As a result of this faulty understanding, many of Nigeria's ethnic groups have been largely hidden from sight over the centuries and received little attention in missionary outreach. Such is the case in numerous other countries as well. Only in the past few decades have we seriously begun to identify these hidden people groups and to concentrate on those groups who have yet to hear.

A significant *mind-shift* must take place throughout the Body of Christ at this point in history if we are to finish *The Great Commission* in this generation. This mind-shift started at the 1974 Lausanne Congress on World Evangelization when the world's mission community began to emphasize that the world should be looked at as people groups rather than as geopolitical countries. That understanding must now work its way throughout the entire Church.

Of course when one begins to look at Scripture closely, God's desire to embrace all of the earth's ethnic groups as worshipers of His glory is clearly seen. As early as Genesis 12, God began unfolding this plan to Abraham. The promise to Abraham, if he would follow and obey God, was two-fold. First, God would bless him and his family abundantly. Second, He would make Abraham a blessing to all the people groups of the earth. Inherent in that revelation was that Abraham would become a "father of nations (people groups)." His descendants would become like the sands of the sea and the stars of the sky. God told Abraham specifically that *all* the families of the earth would be blessed through him and his descendants (Genesis 12:3).

This theme of Jehovah being the God of all the earth's ethnic groups and the object of their worship weaves its way throughout the entirety of the Old Testament. Passages such as Psalm 72:11 capture this: "Yes, all kings shall fall down before Him; all nations [people groups] shall serve Him." Intrinsic in the sending of Messiah would be the blessing of God not only upon Israel, but also upon the Gentiles. Isaiah 42:1–4 says,

> Behold! My Servant whom I uphold, My Elect One in whom My soul delights! I have put My Spirit upon Him; He will bring forth justice to the Gentiles. He will not cry out, nor raise His voice, nor cause His voice to be heard in the street. A bruised reed He will not break, and smoking flax He will not quench; He will bring forth justice for truth. He will not fail nor be discouraged, till He has established justice in the earth; and the coastlands shall wait for His law.

Psalm 22:27 states, "All the ends of the world shall remember and turn to the Lord, and all the families of the nations [people groups] shall worship before You."

The prophet Habakkuk echoed the truth that all peoples are included in God's Kingdom when he declared, "For the earth will be filled with the knowledge of the glory of the LORD, as the waters cover the sea" (Habakkuk 2:14). This thought is, of course, at the very heart of *The Great Commission.* Jesus' clear command to us was to "go therefore and disciple the nations [ethnic groups]" (Matthew 28:19), to "go into all the world and preach the gospel to every creature" (Mark 16:15), and to "be witnesses to Me in Jerusalem, and in all Judea and Samaria, and to the end of the earth" (Acts 1:8).

Worship, the Fuel and Goal of Missions

It is important to understand that God's primary *purpose* for sending His people into the world is not evangelism. Rather it is worship. The primary focus of world evangelization should therefore be the gathering of worshipers of God from each of the world's ethnic groups, rather than simply saving these people from eternal destruction. John Piper reminds us that worship is both the fuel and the goal of missions. Our aim, Piper says, is to bring the nations (people groups) of the earth into "the white-hot enjoyment of God's glory" so that they may fulfill the purpose of their creation (Colossians 1:13–17). Revelation 15:3–4 says,

> Great and marvelous are Your works,
> Lord God Almighty!

Just and true are Your ways, O King of the saints!
Who shall not fear You, O Lord, and glorify Your
name?
For You alone are holy.
For all nations shall come and worship before You,
For Your judgments have been manifested.

Thus, worship is the ultimate goal of missions. But worship is also the fuel for missions, Piper declares. It is our passion to love, worship, and obey God which drives us forward to do what He says and to make whatever sacrifices are necessary to carry out His will in the earth.

The God of Diversity

Before leaving this subject, it should be pointed out that not only is it God's desire that all of the world's people groups should know Him through Christ and become His worshiping followers, but it is also God's wish that each ethnic group should be able to follow Him in the context of its mother culture. More will be written about this later, but we must remember that grave mistakes were made in the past by some missionaries who sought, often unintentionally, to not only make converts but to make converts who looked and acted like converts in their own cultural context. This has, of course, tended to hinder the spontaneous multiplication of churches in new cultures. It is clear from the Scriptures that God loves diversity and that He desires to see that diversity in all elements of the societies which are transformed by the power of the Gospel. Jesus never intended that, as His followers went into the world in obedience to His command, they should make carbon copies of themselves in each new culture they reached.

My purpose in this chapter is not to do an in-depth study of this dream of God for the world, but simply to make it clear that God's vision for the world has, from the beginning, included every people group on earth. His desire is that many representatives from each ethnic group will be worshiping Him forever in heaven. He will not rest until each of these groups has been deeply impacted with the Gospel and until every person in every people group has had opportunity to hear the Gospel message at least one time. Nor should we.

PRACTICAL APPLICATION FOR CHAPTER ONE

1. Meditate on the following statement: "The command of Christ for us to *disciple the nations* (Matthew 28:16–20) is a clear directive to bring the Gospel to every *people group* on earth." (Remember that the term *nations* in the New Testament means "people groups.") Why do you think that, after having *The Great Commission* for 2,000 years, there are more than 6,000 people-groups which are still unreached with the Gospel?

2. Read Genesis 12:1–3 and Genesis 17:1–8. Is it clear to you that God intended that Abraham would indeed become a "father of nations [people groups]" and that *all* the world would be blessed through him, not just Israel? What are the implications of this for missions?

3. Read again Revelation 7:9. Why do you think that

God wants to see representatives around His throne from every nation, tribe, people, and language on the face of the earth? Does it have anything to do with His love for diversity?

4. Think about what was said concerning God's intention for the Gospel to take root in a people group in the context of their *own* culture, instead of in the context of the *missionary's* culture. What are the implications for missionaries today who introduce the Gospel into new cultures?

THE PASSION OF THE CHRIST

"For the Son of Man has come to seek and to save that which was lost."

(Luke 19:10)

In order to illustrate a significant point, there is an important question that should be asked. If the doctors told you that you had only five minutes to live and your family and closest friends were by your bedside, what would you say to them? What would be your *final* words in this world? My guess is that you would not tell them the latest joke you had heard, talk about your favorite sports team, or discuss your current state of health. No, you would not waste your last words, because last words are extremely important. With your last words, you would tell your loved ones whatever it is that is most important to you.

The Last Words of Jesus

Why do I ask that question? Because I wish to illustrate a crucial point and the point is that there was a time when

Jesus had only five minutes left in the world (in His physical body). He had already been crucified, buried, and resurrected by God's power. According to the first chapter of the Acts of the Apostles, Jesus spent the next forty days following His resurrection teaching His disciples about the Kingdom of God (Acts 1:3). He then gathered His closest followers atop the Mount of Olives just outside Jerusalem for His final instructions before leaving to be with the Father. He had five minutes left on the earth. In those five minutes, Jesus did not waste words either. He went straight to the heart of the matter and told His followers the most important thing in the world to Him. With His final words, Jesus shared the passion of His heart. He gave His followers, then and now, *The Great Commission.*

Because the last words of Jesus are so important, I want to give two different accounts of them. The first is the most familiar version of *The Great Commission* given to His disciples in Galilee and found in Matthew 28:18–20:

> And Jesus came and spoke to them saying, "All authority has been given to me in heaven and on earth. Go therefore and make disciples of all the *nations,* baptizing them in the name of the Father and of the Son and of the Holy Spirit, teaching them to observe all things I have commanded you; and lo, I am with you always, even to the end of the age." Amen. (italics added)

This charge from Jesus is very clear. Our directive is to *make disciples* of every *nation* (ethnic group) on earth. And He promised to faithfully accompany us through

His indwelling Holy Spirit as we go in His name to carry out that assignment.

In Acts, chapter 1, we have an additional account of Jesus' final words. The record says,

> And being assembled together with them, He commanded them not to depart from Jerusalem, but to wait for the promise of the Father, "which," He said, "you have heard from me, for John truly baptized with water, but you shall be baptized with the Holy Spirit not many days from now...But you shall receive power when the Holy Spirit has come upon you; and you shall be witnesses to Me in Jerusalem, and in all Judea and Samaria, and to the ends of the earth."
>
> (vv. 4,5,8)

Two things should be noted here. First, Jesus *commanded* His disciples not to leave Jerusalem until they were filled (baptized, anointed, clothed, empowered) with the Holy Spirit. More will be said about this in chapter eight. Suffice it to say for now that Jesus made it clear that His followers would need the Holy Spirit's power in order to be effective witnesses for Him and to be able to significantly change the world through the power of the Gospel. They would not be able to operate successfully in their own strength. Second, it should be emphasized that this baptism (infilling, anointing, clothing, empowering) of the Holy Spirit was given in the *context* of *The Great Commission.* The primary *purpose* of the infilling of the Spirit, according to Jesus' clear statement, was to empower His followers to be capable and powerful witnesses for Him to the world. The Spirit was given to enable people to obey Jesus' orders, to deeply influence the world, and to *finish* the mission He gave us.

The primary point to be made here is that *The Great Commission* was Jesus' *final* directive to His followers. It was the passion of His heart. If anything else had been more important to Him, He certainly would have included it in His departing words. Lest we miss the full significance, we should remember that *The Great Commission* is actually given to us at least *five* times in the New Testament. The fact that God took the time to record this directive from Jesus five different times in His Word should get our attention. Perhaps we can say that in these five separate expressions of the assignment, God wishes for us to see the following:

- Matthew 28:16–20—The *Essence* of *The Great Commission:* Discipling the nations (people groups) of the world.

- Mark 16:14–20—The *Signs* which follow Great Commission preaching: miracles, healings and exorcisms.

- Luke 24:44–49—The *Heart* of Great Commission preaching: repentance and remission of sins to all nations (people groups).

- John 20:19–23—The *Authority* in which Great Commission laborers carry out the mandate: *sent* by Jesus' as His ambassadors in the world.

- Acts 1:4–8—The *Power* for Great Commission workers: the baptism of the Spirit; and the *Strategy* for the expansion of the Kingdom: Jerusalem, Judea, Samaria, and the ends of the earth.

Jesus' Heart for the Nations

The title of this chapter is "The Passion of the Christ." When we normally speak of Christ's passion, we focus on His almost incomprehensible suffering in the events surrounding His crucifixion. That passion, however, is now passed. It was swallowed up in the victory of His resurrection from the dead on that first Easter Sunday. But Christ still lives in Heaven with a passion. The *Passion of the Christ* now is to see His Great Commission orders carried out in full so that the world will be impacted at the deepest level and to see those worshipers from every people group on earth around His throne in eternity. Just as Jesus wept over the residents of Jerusalem because of their failure to recognize Him, surely He is still agonizing over the millions of individuals who have yet to hear of His love and grace. (See Isaiah 53:12; Hebrews 7:25)

This fervor to see the world evangelized was so strong in Jesus that, because the early believers had largely disobeyed His order to take the Gospel to the people groups of the earth, He allowed a strong wave of persecution. This persecution dislodged those first believers from their safety and security in Jerusalem and scattered them throughout Judea and Samaria (Acts 8:1). One thing this early God-action powerfully communicates to us is that Jesus will go to great lengths to motivate His people to finish the assignment He gave us.

The Great Commission a Mandate

Jesus has, in fact, given to His followers a *mandate*. I think we can say without question that in *The Great*

Commission Jesus has given to His followers the most significant directive ever given by anyone in the history of the world. Dr. Ralph Winter, in his superb *Perspectives* course, shows us the significance of a mandate:

> To live under mandate is to be entrusted with a task of lasting significance. Mandates are not commands. By direct commands we assign small errands or daily chores. A mandate, on the other hand, releases authority and responsibility to pursue endeavors of historic importance. God has entrusted to Christ, and with Him to the Church, a mandate to fulfill His purpose for all of history.[1]

Most assuredly, this mandate will be completed. Even though more than one-fourth of the world's population presently lives within people groups where there is no significant church presence, we are certain that they will indeed hear. Earlier I referenced Revelation 7:9. A similar passage is found in Revelation 5:9 where John the Apostle is again privileged to see some of the scenes around God's throne in eternity. There he saw an innumerable host of redeemed people worshiping by singing a new song. It was a song to Jesus and these were its words: "You are worthy to take the scroll and to open its seals; for You were slain, and have redeemed us to God by your blood out of every tribe and tongue and people and nation." To God be the glory! May this passion that is in Jesus to see the *completion* of *The Great Commission* get into each of our hearts and become our passion as well.

In this book I will speak much about the necessity of passion in order to be truly effective in ministry. By *passion* I mean "the joyful abandon of our lives to worship God and to carry out His will and purpose in the world at any cost." Only as this happens—as you and I, together with the rest of God's people across the globe, catch His dream for the world and commit to helping carry out that dream with utter abandon—will we have the vision, the commitment, the passion, and the endurance needed to see Christ's mandate completed.

Practical Application for Chapter Two:

1. Memorize Matthew 28:18–20. Remember that this was Jesus' final instruction to us before leaving to be with the Father.

2. Why do you think God took the time and effort to record *The Great Commission* five times in the New Testament? Write out your answer.

3. Is the finishing of *The Great Commission* a passion within *you?* If not, why not? If so, how is it being demonstrated in your life?

4. Spend some personal time in prayer now, asking God to truly capture your heart with this vision to see *The Great Commission* completed in this generation.

Endnotes

1 *Perspectives*, Ralph Winter, ed., 1999 Edition, p. 81

UNDERSTANDING THE MISSIONARY TASK

"Declare His glory among the nations, His wonders among all peoples."

(Psalm 96:3)

My desire is that this book will be both inspirational and instructional. The writing contains several inspiring testimonies and examples of what God is doing in different parts of the world. Also, for the sake of clarity, we must have a common understanding that will help facilitate our desire to finish *The Great Commission* in this generation. Following are several definitions of key terms[1] which should be grasped by the reader before we proceed. A common understanding of these missionary terms will help us to communicate more effectively as the writing unfolds.

The Great Commission—"The work of the church in discipling believers in Jerusalem, Judea, Samaria, and the ends of the earth." This is, of course, the heart of our study. It is essential that readers understand that this term has, along with the others which follow, a precise definition. Each word is important and the definition should be meditated on until it is clearly comprehended.

Especially note that the essence of Jesus' command here is to *disciple* the nations, not simply to evangelize them. This will be discussed more fully in chapter nine, but for now we should keep in mind that there is much more to making disciples than winning people to Christ. Converts must also be taught, as Jesus told us, "to observe all things I have commanded you" (Matthew 28:20). We must remember that new believers do not *automatically* become powerful followers of Jesus. They must be taught quickly, clearly, simply, without excess religious baggage, and in the context of their own culture, how to follow Christ and what it means to be His disciple.

Also, we are reminded by this definition that the work of discipling believers is to be done throughout the entire earth. Let us keep in mind that this command to disciple each of the world's ethnic groups is given to all believers everywhere, not only to those in the Western world. In fact, each local church or church planting organization, wherever it is located in the world and of whomever it is comprised, is commissioned by Jesus to be resolute about this task.

Missions—"The cross-cultural work of The Great Commission." If the essence of *The Great Commission* is to disciple all the ethnic groups of the earth, then it must include the discipling both of people who are like us in language and culture and also of people who are different from us. Work done among our own people group, whichever group that may be, is called "evangelism." Work done among ethnic groups which are significantly different from our own is called "missions."

Missionary—"A person who enters another culture or ethnic group in order to make disciples." If *The Great Commission* is indeed to be completed, then every follower of Christ and every church on earth must be focused, at least to some extent, on this issue. Thousands of cross-cultural missionaries are needed around the world for the job to be completed and tens of thousands of churches are needed to train, send, and assist them in their work.

From the outset of this writing, it must be clearly understood that all *missionaries* do not have white skin. Whether or not one is a missionary has nothing at all to do with the color of his skin. In fact, even now, the *majority* of the world's missionaries do not have white skin. They have brown skin, black skin, yellow skin, or red skin—and a wide range of each color. These are the missionaries who will play the central role in finishing *The Great Commission*. More will be discussed about this later also, but it is vital to understand that the leadership of missions in the world is changing hands. It is quickly moving and, to a considerable extent, already has moved from the West to the nations of the Two-Thirds World.

People group—"A group of people who share common ethnic, cultural, and linguistic traits." The awareness that the world's population is divided into distinct people groups has come into clearer focus in the Body of Christ in general and to missions in particular during the past few decades. This awareness has been helpful in understanding how *The Great Commission* can and will be completed. The realization that the specific command of Jesus was for His followers to "disciple the *nations*" (people groups) of the world has also given us a better understanding of the portion of the task which remains. Presently, *Joshua Project* identifies 9,599 distinct people groups in the world (15,874 in all, when each group is counted separately in each country). These ethnic groups include, for example, the Bhojpuri people of India, the Khmer people of Cambodia, the Burmese people of Myanmar (Burma), several Hispanic groups of Central and South America, the Hausa people of Nigeria, the Kurdish people of Turkey, and the Bengali people of Bangladesh and India, just to mention a few. It is important to understand that these people groups which are unreached with the Gospel must become, as Dr. Howard Foltz suggests, "the strategic target of missions." As we reach and disciple each of these people groups for Christ, we will fulfill God's vision for the world and finish *The Great Commission.*

Unreached Peoples—"Ethnic groups in which most of their constituents live their entire lives without ever hearing an understandable presentation of the Gospel." At the time of this writing, *Joshua Project* lists 6,417 people groups as being *unreached* with the Gospel. Sometimes they are referred to as *hidden peoples* or *least-reached* peoples. Although different organizations number and define these unreached ethnic groups differently, the important thing to understand is that, after having *The Great Commission* for 2,000 years, more than two billion people have had virtually no exposure to the Gospel.[2]

In missiological terms, an *unreached* people group (UPG) means an ethnic group which is less than 2% evangelical (born-again) and less than 5% in total Christian adherents. The general thought is that once a people group reaches 2% evangelical, it has reached a point where it has sufficient numbers and resources to evangelize its own people. Until that time the group must have significant help from missionaries and other outside groups and organizations for its people to be reached with the Gospel. We must, however, be very careful from the beginning not to create a dependency on any of these outside groups which will hinder the free flow of the Gospel among the people group being reached and the rapid multiplication of new churches among them.

In order to finish our task, these *Unreached Peoples* must be specifically targeted for church planting. Herein is a significant problem. More about this will be discussed later but, for now, let's simply understand that the vast majority of missions resources (people, money, thinking, literature, etc.) are focused on people groups which are already "reached" by missiological definition. Out of the current global missionary force of 420,000, only about 10,000 (2.3%) of them are working among the world's least-reached peoples.[3] In order to finish *The Great Commission,* there must be a major readjustment of missions assets. We must intentionally and strategically target people groups which are unreached for evangelism and church planting.

Closure—"The concept that The Great Commission can be completed in a measurable way by establishing a viable, indigenous, evangelizing Church Planting Movement among every people-group on earth." This is our goal and it is to this end that we must labor with all diligence. This indeed must become our passion if we are to finish *The Great Commission* in this generation. It is my prayer and hope that this objective will capture the heart of the Church of Jesus Christ in the twenty-first century.

It will not suffice just to have a missionary laboring among each people group. Nor will it be adequate to simply have a church or a number of churches planted among each of these *Unreached Peoples.* In order to bring *closure* to *The Great Commission,* each people group needs to have a viable, indigenous group of churches which is rapidly reproducing among them.

A Great Commission Church—"A church which teaches its people and organizes its ministries to help fulfill The Great Commission in this generation." In order to finish the assignment Jesus gave us, the world must become filled with *Great Commission Churches.* Thousands and thousands of churches in every country on earth must become focused on this mission. The prayer gatherings, cell groups, house church meetings, women's ministries, youth and children's ministries, evangelism and missions outreaches, financial operations, and every other ministry of the church much catch the vision of reaching the world for Christ. Without this, we cannot finish the mission.

A Great Commission Believer—"A believer who organizes his life and family around helping to fulfill the Great Commission." Only as individual believers get serious about obeying Jesus' command in their daily lives and teach it to their families can we build the *Great Commission Churches* just referenced. The church is not comprised of brick and mortar; it is made up of flesh and blood. The church is not primarily a building or an organization. Rather it is a body of believers which consists of people who are covenanted together in a given location to be the Body of Christ in that area. In order to finish *The Great Commission,* more and more believers must allow the heart of Jesus for lost people to become their hearts also. They must be committed in their praying, in their giving, and in their going to disciple the world's remaining unreached millions.

A Church Planting Movement—"A rapid multiplication of indigenous churches planting churches that sweeps through a people group or population segment."[4] All over the world God is using *Church Planting Movements* to quickly multiply both believers and churches and to advance *The Great Commission* at rates which were formerly unthinkable. These movements are often characterized by the following: 1) a people group focus; 2) the translation of the Bible in the mother tongue (heart language) of the group; 3) rapid development of indigenous leadership; 4) financial self-support by the group; 5) house churches or cell groups which are small in number and which can be multiplied quickly; 6) evangelistic and missionary initiative; 7) churches planting other churches; and 8) unpaid, non-professional leadership of the individual cells or house churches. Until there are such movements among all of the world's *Unreached Peoples,* the mandate Christ has given will not be completed.

An Indigenous Church—"A native or home-grown church movement (as opposed to a foreign or alien one) which is familiar to, comfortable for, and led by the people group being reached." Throughout the history of Protestant missions, there have been great successes and accomplishments which have impacted societies all over the world and been a source of enormous blessing. At the same time there have been unfortunate errors of judgment or lack of understanding by some missionaries which have retarded the progress of God's work among those civilizations to which they were sent. If we are to finish *The Great Commission,* we must learn from those mistakes. We must make sure that new works started among *Unreached Peoples* are done in a way that does not compromise the essence of the Gospel, that makes for the rapid advancement of God's Kingdom among them, and which is void of the "excess baggage" missionaries often bring from their own cultures. It is vital that the new works which are begun be self-governing, self-supporting, and self-propagating.

The principal objective of this book is to help churches and believers around the world catch the vision for finishing *The Great Commission* in this generation—and for impacting the world around them in the process. In order to complete the task, the world must be filled with *Great Commission Churches* and *Great Commission Believers* and must see thousands of *Church Planting Movements* launched among the world's least-reached peoples. May God grant that this will happen quickly, and may He use this book as a catalyst to help see the task completed in this generation.

Practical Application for Chapter Three:

1. Read again each of the definitions given in this chapter. Think about each one as you read it. Make sure that you understand each definition clearly.

2. Think about the definition of the word *closure*. Have you ever thought seriously about seeing *The Great Commission* finished in your lifetime?

3. What do you know about the *Unreached Peoples* who are located in your state or country? Can you name any of those groups? Write down as many as you can think of.

4. Think about the definition of a *Great Commission Church*. What do you think it would take to make *your* church a *Great Commission Church?* What can you do personally to help this effort?

5. Read again the definition of a *Church Planting Movement* and an *Indigenous Church*. What are some of the things, in your opinion, which have hindered the rapid development of the Church among some societies in the past? Write down your answers.

Endnotes

1 I am indebted to Dr. Howard Foltz and his AIMS teachings, especially his *"Harvest Connection"* training, and to Dr. David Garrison, for clarity in several of these definitions.

2 U. S. Center for World Mission.

3 *Perspectives*, Ralph Winter, ed., 1999 edition, p. 249.

4 *Church Planting Movements* (Dr. David Garrison; WIGTake Resources, Midlothian, VA, 2004)

A Tale of Two
Churches

"Let your light so shine before men, that they may see
your good works and glorify your Father in heaven."
(Matthew 5:16)

Let me tell you a simple but true story of two churches. In some ways these two churches are similar, but in
other ways they are vastly different. The first church is
an ordinary church. There are thousands of churches
like it all over the world. Ordinary churches normally
make no significant impact on and have little influence
in the cities, towns, and villages where they are located.
In fact, they often do not influence much of anything.
They are ordinary churches. But the second church
I wish to describe is enormously different. It is what
I call a "Great Commission Church" (or an "Impact
Church"). There are not many of them around, but
they are powerful in that they make a genuine difference for Christ in their spheres of influence. They challenge their cultures, win many people to Jesus, successfully disciple new believers, effectively minister to the

needs of their communities, plant new churches, help reach those who have not heard, and make the world a better place to live. Now here's the story of the two churches.

An Ordinary Church

The first church is found in one of the world's major cities. For fifteen years the congregation had been meeting in a particular part of that city. Not much of significance was happening. Few people were being won to Christ in the church's neighborhood and no effective outreach ministries to the community were in operation. The members met in a church building but not one of good quality. One day this church was offered the opportunity to buy a nicer church building which was located in a totally different part of their city. Both the leadership and the members agreed that they should buy the new building, so they did. The new building was located a considerable distance away from their previous building in a totally different community.

After moving to the new location, the pastor wanted to discover what impact his congregation had made on the community where they had previously been located for fifteen years. So he developed a plan. Several of the church members were trained to go door-to-door and ask key questions of the people in the area. For several weeks they talked to people in their former community and asked the questions that had been formulated. Then the church leadership tallied the answers to the questions in order to determine the church's impact on their former neighborhood.

Do you know what they found? They found that

the church had made no measurable impact at all. For fifteen years they had met regularly in that community but largely, they determined, to no avail. The leaders came to understand, in fact, that the people of the area had not even realized the congregation had moved out of their community to the new location! They didn't even realize they were gone from the neighborhood. Perhaps, if that were the case, the community was never really conscious that the church was there in the first place. This church knew or practiced little which would help bring the transforming power of God's Kingdom into its community. They were just an ordinary church and, as we said, the world is full of them.

Ordinary churches regularly have a limited and rather self-centered view of ministry. They tend to live with a "maintenance mentality," focusing on their own members and having little heart for the world around them. Just as the leaders of the Protestant Reformation (Calvin, Luther, Zwingli, etc.) had good theology but little, if any, theology of mission,[1] the leaders of these churches have eyes which focus primarily on themselves. They have not understood that Jesus came to seek and to save lost people and that He has commissioned His followers to do likewise. This is one of the primary reasons they often do not grow and do not exert significant influence in the world around them.

An Extraordinary Church

The story of our second church is different—hugely different. This is a church which is also located in one of the world's major cities. In some ways it looks to the untrained eye much like the church just described. But a closer look at this congregation reveals that it is, in fact, vastly different. This church impacts its community at a deep level. Hundreds of people from the neighborhood and from surrounding neighborhoods are being won to Christ. Baptisms take place on a weekly basis. New converts are discipled to become powerful followers of Jesus. A number of prostitutes, drug addicts, and gang members have become followers of Jesus. Several of their members formerly spent time in prison but had their lives totally changed through the power of the Gospel. Some had been gang leaders and some involved in organized crime. Several of these former leaders in crime have become leaders in the church. The church also has numerous effective outreach ministries to the poor, to gangs, and to prostitutes in their neighborhood. In addition, they are learning about the *Unreached Peoples* of the world and are beginning to gain a heart for reaching those who have not heard.

This church is, in fact, so influential in its community that the mayor of the city came on one occasion to present the church with an award. The mayor thanked the church for being such a positive influence in the district and informed them that the rate of crime in their part of the city had been significantly reduced because of their presence. How the world needs more churches like this one—churches which indeed help to bring God's Kingdom to the earth and help to transform society at its deepest levels. (See Note 1 in the Appendix for additional comments on the Kingdom of God.)

An Important Query

Which of these two churches would you like *your* church to be like? I have asked this question in meetings with pastors and church leaders all over the world. Not once have I seen a leader who wanted his church to be like the first church described. No, we all want to be a part of something significant. We want our churches to make a genuine difference in the world. The remainder of this book focuses on *how* to build these *Great Commission Churches*–churches which do indeed impact the world around them as they seek to help finish *The Great Commission* in this generation. On the pages which follow you will find helpful insight on how to build these *Impact Churches.* In my travels and observations in more than forty nations of the world, I have identified ten major characteristics of churches which change their worlds. These ten distinctives will be discussed at length. We will look at each characteristic both philosophically and practically in order to clearly understand why and how these *Great Commission Churches* are making a difference and are helping to bring God's Kingdom to the families, communities, people groups, and countries of the world. Our goal is to help you to unmistakably understand these qualities and gain practical insight on how to incorporate them into your church or organization.

PRACTICAL APPLICATION FOR CHAPTER FOUR:

1. Think about the two churches described in this chapter. What characteristics can you identify which made

the second church significantly different from the first? Write down your answers.

2. Do you personally know any churches that you would describe as *Great Commission Churches* (*Impact Churches*)? If so, what are their distinguishing characteristics? Take time to list the qualities that you think would qualify those churches as *Great Commission Churches*.

3. Does your church have any effective outreach ministries to your community? If so, what makes them effective? What kinds of lasting results are you seeing?

4. If your church is more like the first church described, please ask God now how you might personally contribute to helping your church become a *Great Commission Church*.

ENDNOTES

1 *Breaking Tradition to Accomplish Vision*, Paul R. Gupta and Sherwood G. Lingelfelter, (BMH Books: Winona Lake, IN, 2006), p. 81.

SENSE OF DESTINY

THE FIRST CHARACTERISTIC OF GREAT COMMISSION CHURCHES

"I, therefore, the prisoner of the Lord, beseech you to walk worthy of the calling with which you were called."

(Ephesians 4:1)

In order to finish *The Great Commission* in this generation, the world must be filled with tens of thousands of new churches. The need, however, is not for ordinary churches–churches which have little influence on the communities around them. Rather the need is for *Great Commission Churches* which serve as salt and light in society and help to bring God's Kingdom to the peoples of the earth. This is the real answer for world evangelization. With many more of these *Impact Churches,* we can indeed change the world and finish the assignment Jesus gave us.

The first characteristic of churches which change the world is that they have a "sense of destiny." Let me explain. By "sense of destiny" I mean that these churches and church planting organizations have a strong awareness that there is a divine *call* from God upon them as a church or organization to participate with Him in building His Kingdom. Both the leaders and the members are cognizant of the fact that they are not an ordinary church. Rather, they have an inner awareness that they are partnering with God to do something significant in the world. They understand they are the *Body of Christ* in their communities.

In all of my observations and reading, I have never encountered a church of major influence anywhere in the world which did not have this characteristic. Nor have I met or read of an individual who helped significantly to shape the world who did not have this trait. Let me remind you of John Wesley, founder of the *Methodist* movement; Hudson Taylor, the missionary statesman to China; Mother Teresa of Calcutta; Evangelist Billy Graham; and William Booth, founder of the *Salvation Army*. Also think about certain political leaders such as Mahatma Gandhi of India and Martin Luther King, Jr. of the United States. What did these people have in common? To be sure, they had many things in common. But one trait they shared was a *sense of destiny*. Each of them was aware that there was a strong *call* of some kind upon his or her life. (See Note 2 in the Appendix for further comments about the call of God.) They had been given a song to sing to the world and they knew it. They knew they were created for a purpose and they dedicated themselves to that purpose which was larger than their own lives.

Jesus' Sense of Destiny

Jesus was aware of such a calling upon His own life as a

child. An interesting story is told of Jesus when He was twelve years of age (Luke 2:41–50). His family had journeyed from Nazareth to Jerusalem for the Passover Feast, one of the primary Jewish festivals. When the festivities were ended, the family began traveling back home. In those days people often traveled in large groups or caravans comprised of many relatives, friends, and neighbors. As they left to return to Nazareth, Mary and Joseph thought that Jesus was in the caravan. When they discovered that He was not in the group, they quickly returned to Jerusalem to look for Him. Surprisingly they found Him in the Temple area discoursing with doctors and lawyers. After a slight rebuke from His parents, Jesus responded: "Why did you seek me? Did you not know that I must be about My Father's business?"

This is a good example of a *sense of destiny*. Even at twelve years of age, Jesus was aware that He was not an ordinary child. He knew that He was on a mission for His Father. Churches which change the world and help to bring peace, justice, and hope to their communities are like that. Both their leaders and their members are aware that they are collaborating with God to do something of genuine significance in their communities.

The Need for a Sense of Destiny

Without this *sense of destiny*, churches and organizations generally will not be able to sustain the strength needed to become a church of significant influence. Building churches which impact the world is not an easy task. It requires much prayer, vision, insight, wisdom, and determined effort over a prolonged period of time. Without a *sense of destiny*, churches generally cannot and will not pay the price required to deeply impact villages, towns, and cities. Nor will they have the passion essential to do so.

Without this *sense of destiny,* congregations will not be able to stand for long in the midst of persecution. All over the world followers of Jesus are being required to pay a great price for influence. Often that price involves beatings, being ostracized from family, imprisonment, and sometimes even death. Such has always been the case. Indeed, "the blood of martyrs is the seed of the church." Without the awareness that they are specially called of God to do something of significance, the church will often lose heart and give up in times of suffering. It is, in fact, this *sense of destiny* which largely enables them to carry on with joy in the midst of extreme difficulty.

Sense of Destiny and Leadership

One other word about this is essential. In order to impact the world, a church must raise up quality leaders who will help carry the church to its future. Training other leaders is one of our most important leadership responsibilities. Without this deep awareness of God's calling and destiny, churches often are not able to retain good leaders. Soon their young leaders are off to start churches on their own or to connect with other churches or organizations which do have a *sense of destiny. Great Commission Churches,* however, are regularly able to keep the majority of the leaders they raise up. They also often attract good leaders from other churches and organizations. Quality leaders want to be a part of something significant. They will normally not waste their time with the ordinary.

Jesus was able to attract, train, and keep quality leaders. It is interesting to note that, upon the initiation of His public ministry, one of the first things Jesus did was to call people to join Him in His mission. Fishermen, tax collectors, political zealots—people from all walks of life were called to leave their occupations in order to follow Him. What I find amazing is that these people actually walked off their jobs, and sometimes left family businesses, in order to link up with Jesus. Why would they do that? These were not children playing a game. Why would adult fishermen leave their trades or a tax collector forsake significant wealth in order to follow an itinerant teacher? The answer is, in part, because they saw this *sense of destiny* in Jesus.

A few years ago a song was written about Jesus which said, "He has fire in His eyes and a sword in His hand, and He's riding a white horse across the land—and He's calling out to you and me, 'Will you ride with me?'" I love the words of the song which follow: "Yes, Lord. We will ride."[1] That's it! These people left their jobs and followed Him because they were linking with Someone who "had fire in His eyes"—Someone who knew that He was on a mission for God to change the world. And they wanted to be part of that mission.

This should not surprise us. People are, in fact, still doing the same today. As I traverse the globe, I find people everywhere who are making great sacrifices in order to become a part of something significant—in order to make their lives count for something eternal. Organizations such as *Youth With A Mission, Operation Mobilization,* and *Campus Crusade for Christ,* along with many indigenous groups in countries all over the world, are living proofs of this. In these ministries, hundreds of people each year, many of them professional people, quit their jobs or take early retirement in order to link up with them. Why? Because, like Jesus' disciples, they want to be a part of something that is changing the world. The same is happening in *Great Commission Churches* all over the world. Business leaders are leaving secular positions in order to lead ministries in their churches. Some are coming on as paid staff. Others are volunteering. Why? Because almost everyone wants to be a part of something momentous.

How to Gain a Sense of Destiny

Now here's an important question: How does this *sense of destiny* get into the life of a church or an organization? How does one go about transferring that quality to a group which does not already possess it? The answer is that it must come through the pastor or the primary leader of the group. This key leader is, in reality, the *only* vehicle through which this quality can come to a congregation. No other leader in the church can do it. If the pastor or primary leader has a *sense of destiny,* the church can catch it. If he does not, the church will never get it. So, if that is the case, how does a pastor or leader go about finding this quality? If he does not already have it, how can he obtain it? Let me answer by stating that, if the senior leader is not already aware of this *sense of destiny,* it will come only by seeking God with his whole heart. (See such passages as Jeremiah 29:13 and Matthew 7:7,8.) God promises each of us that if we seek Him wholeheartedly, we will find Him. This quality comes to leaders who fast, pray, and deeply reflect on their purpose in life. It comes as they seriously wrestle with this issue and receive clear revelation from the Holy Spirit concerning their purpose and calling in life. A *sense of destiny* comes from spending much time alone with God and asking Him to clearly reveal it.

John Wesley was one of the world's greatest leaders. Few people could match him in his ability to train other quality leaders in the Body of Christ. His ministry impacted nations. Wesley referred to himself from time to time as "a brand plucked from the burning." What did he mean by that? This was a reference to a time during his early childhood when he was trapped in the family home which was burning to the ground. It appeared that Wesley would die in the flames, but somehow God miraculously spared his life. Wesley's reason, however, for using this term was that he understood that God "plucked him from the burning" for a purpose. God spared him because He had put destiny in John Wesley's life. That destiny, I submit, is in the life of *every* person, including you.

If I were a pastor or key leader who wanted to turn my church or organization into a *Great Commission Church,* I would do one thing. If I did not have this *sense of destiny* burning strongly inside me, I would get on my face before God and discover the reason for my life. Just as Jacob wrestled with the angel, I would lay hold of God and not let Him go until I clearly understood my destiny and calling in life and until that calling became an intense passion inside me. Then I would preach and teach this truth to my congregation or group until a *sense of destiny* gripped the entire church or group and worked its way into the breadth and depth of the church's consciousness.

Examples of Sense of Destiny

One prime example of this *sense of destiny* is the amazing Saddleback Church in Southern California (USA) which is led by Pastor Rick Warren.[2] Saddleback is widely recognized as not only one of the world's largest but also one of the truly influential churches. Indeed Saddleback is a *Great Commission Church* which is impacting its community for Christ and helping spread the Gospel around the world. Pastor Warren certainly seems to have been able to build this sense of destiny into the heart and soul of his congregation. And he has done it in significant part through casting a captivating vision for church members. In his very first sermon to his newly formed congregation, Pastor Warren shared a gripping vision which resonated with his people. (See Note 3 in the Appendix for a copy of Rick Warren's original vision.) Although there is not a clear statement in Pastor Warren's written vision about reaching those who have not heard, it is apparent that his congregation is now doing so in many significant ways. The vision statement would have been stronger, in my opinion, had it also included a clear vision for reaching out to the world's *Unreached Peoples*. Rick is a wise pastor who understands that one of the primary ways a leader builds a *sense of destiny* into the life of a congregation is by helping people to personally take ownership of a significant vision. Indeed it is this captivating vision (and the congregation taking ownership of it) which brings this *sense of destiny* into the life of a church.

The *Congregacao Crista no Brasil* is another example of a congregation which has a *sense of destiny*. Author William R. Read, in his book entitled *New Patterns of*

Church Growth in Brazil, gives insight into the *sense of destiny* of this dynamic congregation:

> A certain mentality has grown up around the prophecy of their founder that the Church has a divinely inspired "particular" mission to fulfill. Members think of the Congregacao as an agency of the Lord at a particular time and place in the work of harvesting....This has a psychological effect upon the whole Church. It creates an atmosphere of expectancy. It aids growth and progress. If God is for us, who can be against us.[3]

Your Personal Sense of Destiny

Leaders who change the world are impact people. They change things. Impact people see large visions and dream big dreams. They develop a vision and a passion to do something significant for God—something which effectively captures their hearts. They no longer dream about what might happen or what could happen. Rather they become convinced that these things *must* happen. They also effectively communicate this vision to their congregations or organizations through their preaching and teaching. The result is a *sense of destiny* which develops within the hearts of their followers.

But what about you? What kind of vision do you have for your city or town or village? Are you partnering with God to change the world or are you, in your own mind, just another pastor or leader? Are you aware of the divine call of God that is upon your life and your church? As the Scriptures affirm that John the Baptist was "a man sent from God," (John 1:6) do you also have the keen perception that you have been sent by God into the world to do something specific? Are you communicating that effectively to your people? Ferdinand Foch has said that "the most powerful weapon on earth is the human soul on fire." That's what a *sense of destiny* breeds in the lives of people. It sets their soul on fire for something—something significant. So here's a parting question for this discussion: What is it that sets *your* soul on fire? What are you living for? What passion is inside you? Oliver Wendell Holmes once said that "sooner or later life will come down to the question of how much fire you have in your belly." How much fire do you have? If such a fire is not presently burning inside you, are you willing to do what it takes to find it?

PRACTICAL APPLICATION FOR CHAPTER FIVE:

1. On a separate sheet of paper write your understanding of a *sense of destiny.* Read again the first part of chapter five. Does the description you wrote adequately explain the term?

2. Would you say that you have a clear *sense of destiny* in your own life? Do you understand that the call of God is heavy upon you personally? If so, what has God called you to do with your life? Please take time now to write your answer. (If you are not clear about this, why not set aside an extended time of fasting and prayer to get alone with God and find out why you are in the world? In the spirit of Jacob wrestling with the

angel, refuse to let God go until you have heard from Him in your heart concerning this matter.)

3. What are some practical things that you can do to help your church or organization gain a *sense of destiny?* Take time to write out your answer. Review this chapter if needed.

Endnotes

1   *"We Will Ride"* written and recorded by Brownsville Revival

2   Pastor Rick Warren's outstanding book *The Purpose Driven Church* (Zondervan Publishing House) captures the story of this dynamic church. This book is well worth reading.

3   Grant McClung, ed. *Azusa Street and Beyond* (Gainsville, Fl: Bridge-Logos, 2006). p. 85

PERSEVERANCE IN PRAYER AND INTERCESSION

THE SECOND CHARACTERISTIC OF GREAT COMMISSION CHURCHES

"So I say to you, ask, and it will be given to you; seek, and you will find; knock, and it will be opened to you.

(Luke 11:9)

The second characteristic of churches which change the world is that they persevere in prayer and intercession. These churches know the power of prayer, they know how to pray, and they pray. With them prayer is not simply a religious exercise. It is their heart and soul. These *Impact Churches* do three things consistently and passionately:

They intercede for people who do not know Christ—and they do so in a variety of ways. Some of their wise leaders regularly take a few minutes out of their worship gatherings to ask their members to cry out to God for lost family and friends, using their

Evangelistic Prayer List (A simple way to intercede for lost loved ones. This will be discussed in the following chapter.) or some other suitable method. They do this also in their specialized gatherings—in leadership meetings, cell group meetings, women's meetings, prayer services, youth and children's meetings—and they do so because prayer is a *priority* with them. They genuinely believe God will hear and answer their prayers. In so doing these leaders are helping to impart vision for evangelism in their churches.

The second church described in chapter four (the one which deeply impacted its community and helped to bring God's Kingdom) has regular prayer emphases when the entire church gathers to pray for the unsaved. Once every three months this church has a "Prayer Revival." For an entire week church members fast and pray. They gather each evening during that week to humble themselves before God. The entire evening is devoted to prayer and a significant part of that prayer time is given to intercession for the lost. This church is serious about prayer and serious about praying for unconverted family, friends, and neighbors—and they regularly reap the rewards of such prayer as people surrender their lives to Christ.

They intercede for the world's unreached millions. Churches which change the world not only have a burden for their own cities and towns; they also have a burden for those who have yet to hear. Because they are zealous to see *The Great Commission* completed, they take time in their special prayer gatherings, and sometimes in their regular worship services, to pray for the world's remaining 6,000 unreached people groups, and especially for the group or groups which they are personally targeting for church planting ministry. These churches understand that, if we are to finish *The Great Commission* in this generation, the world's *Unreached Peoples* must be specifically and individually targeted both for prayer and church planting.

They intercede for more laborers to enter the harvest. *Great Commission Churches* understand clearly what Jesus said in Matthew 9:37–38: "The harvest truly is plentiful, but the laborers are few. Therefore pray the Lord of the harvest to send out laborers into His harvest." These churches realize there is indeed a spiritual harvest going on around the world and that more workers are needed to reap it. Almost everywhere I travel in the Two-Thirds World, I see this harvest in progress. Indeed, there is nothing wrong with the harvest. The only problem, as Jesus clearly showed us, is insufficient laborers to bring in the harvest. Churches which change the world believe and practice what Jesus said. They understand, as veteran missionary Robert E. Speer reiterates, "Missions work has been least fruitful when the church has prayed the least. The evangelization of the world in this generation depends on a revival of prayer." So it does. If we are to finish *The Great Commission* in this generation, we must have thousands of churches rise to the challenge of prayer and intercede faithfully, passionately, and persistently for the discipling of the world's remaining *Unreached Peoples.* We must hear what Jesus is saying and not allow the ripened harvest to go unreaped due to a lack of laborers. As these churches pray for laborers, they also make themselves available to answer the call.

An amazing promise is given to God's followers in Psalm 2:8: "Ask of Me, and I will give You the nations for Your inheritance, and the ends of the earth for Your possession." It is important to understand that this was not only a prophetic promise given to Jesus; it was also given to Jesus' followers—the *Body of Christ* on the earth. Churches which impact their worlds ask God for the *nations* (people groups) which are presently unreached with the Gospel. They understand, as Oswald Chambers has so aptly said, "Prayer does not *equip* us for the battle; prayer *is* the battle." These churches know the crucial battles of life and ministry are fought and won in prayer. May more of God's people around the world learn this lesson—that believing prayer is the really hard work and that ministry is simply gathering up the results of those prayers!

Andrew Murray soberly reminds us that God, by creating man with a free will and making him a partner in the rule of the earth, has, to some extent, chosen to limit Himself. He has in fact made Himself somewhat dependent on man's obedient response to His will and commands. God desires and delights to show Himself strong and powerful in the earth. For this reason He regularly calls out to His people with such appeals as, "Call to Me, and I will answer you, and show you great and mighty things, which you do not know" (Jeremiah 33:3). However, when God's people do not call to Him and trust Him to do these great and mighty things, He often does not do them. Passages such as Ezekiel 22:30–31 appear to bear this out. Here God says,

"So I sought for a man among them who would make a wall, and stand in the gap before me on behalf of the land, that I should not destroy it; but I found none. Therefore I have poured out My indignation on them; I have consumed them with the fire of My wrath; and I have recompensed their deeds on their own heads," says the Lord.

It is clear in this passage that God's desire was to spare Jerusalem and that this desire was so strong that He actually sought after people to intercede for the city. However, because He could find no one to intervene in prayer on Israel's behalf, His wrath was poured out on Jerusalem. *Great Commission Churches* recognize these things and repeatedly cry out to God in earnest prayer and intercession for His power to be released.

Revival in Korea

One of the most remarkable stories of church history is the revival that impacted South Korea in the twentieth century. It is difficult to comprehend that at the beginning of the century there was almost no church presence in South Korea, and yet, by the end of the century, the country was almost 30% born again. Seldom, if ever, has the world seen a revival of such magnitude and one which so deeply impacted a country. It is interesting that, not only is the largest church in the world today (700,000 members at the time of this writing) located in South Korea, but *several* of the world's largest churches are there. Amazingly, there are now nearly 5,000 churches in the capital city of Seoul alone.

Why is this? How can a country go from almost

zero to 30% born again in one century? Such is possible only through the power of believing prayer. I remember reading a number of years ago about a news reporter's interview with a pastor in South Korea. The reporter asked the pastor how such a remarkable revival had occurred in his country. His answer was, "Because we have shifted the principalities." This pastor was saying an incredible spiritual victory had been won in the heavenlies over South Korea. The statement reminds us of Paul's insight into spiritual warfare: "For we do not wrestle against flesh and blood, but against principalities, against powers, against the rulers of the darkness of this age, against spiritual hosts of wickedness in the heavenly places" (Ephesians 6:12).

Granted, some people may have taken this truth of warring against evil, controlling, spiritual powers to extremes, but it is vital to remember that it is indeed a truth. Paul clearly tells us that Jesus' followers have been given powerful spiritual weapons for the pulling down of the enemy's strongholds (See 2 Corinthians 10:3–5). South Korea, along with most other countries of the world, was dominated for centuries by wicked spiritual powers which controlled and manipulated the thoughts of the masses, and often the leaders of the country. These forces kept South Korea bound in Buddhism and other forms of spiritual darkness for generations. Paul reminds us we are to war against such controlling powers—and this warring is done principally through prayer and intercession. Bold, aggressive, unrelenting spiritual warfare on the part of God's people is often essential to diminish the strength of these spiritual forces and displace them. For decades,

Jesus' followers in South Korea obeyed Paul's injunction and interceded for their country. *Prayer Mountains* were built all across the country where believers could go for days or weeks at a time to fast and pray. And to these places of intercession they did go—by the hundreds and thousands.

Through God's grace, the church in South Korea has been built on a rock-solid foundation of prayer and intercession. The result was that God's people in South Korea "prayed a hole through the sky," so to speak. Their intercession broke through the heavenlies and, to some extent, dethroned those evil spiritual forces which had held their nation captive for ages. In answer to prayer the spiritual "blinders" were removed from the eyes of the people (See 2 Corinthians 4:3–4) and revival came to South Korea. Recently I was in a Korean church in the USA. The pastor told me that I was to speak five times during the weekend and that one of those meetings would be a Saturday morning prayer service at 5:30 a.m. Approximately 100 people were there on that early Saturday morning (and every Saturday morning) to pray. Evidently, the effects of the Korean church's early prayer habits are widespread still.

How the Church of Jesus Christ needs to learn this lesson! Someone once said that the only thing we learn from history is that we don't learn from history. Will God's people learn anything from South Korea's history of prayer and intercession? Will Jesus' followers in the countries and among the people groups of the world learn to unite in fervent, believing prayer in order to bring down the principalities and powers that tend to rule their societies as the Koreans have done? Or will we continue with "business as usual?" This is an important question. It is apparent the church in India is learning this lesson. Recently, on a *Pentecost Sunday,* more than 500,000 believers were mobilized across the country for a day of intercession as a part of the *Global Day of Prayer.* It is no wonder that some 10,000 people per day are reportedly coming to Christ in India at present.

The Fall of Communism

Prayer emphases like this offer much hope for the world. Many followers of Christ believe that the fall of communism, illustrated so vividly by the demolishing of the *Berlin Wall* which separated East and West Berlin, was the result of powerful intercession on the part of believers around the world. Only eternity will reveal the truth of such things, but suffice it to say that believing prayer is, without question, the most powerful force on earth. Through such prayer, Jesus declared "all things are possible to him who believes" (Mark 9:23). The greatest need, however, is for individuals, local churches, and groups and organizations all over the world to rediscover this prayer potential and to become *Houses of Prayer* which intercede regularly for their communities, their towns, their cities, and for the world's unreached millions.

Prayer and Church Planting Movements

In his book entitled *Church Planting Movements,* David Garrison relates a story of a particular *Church Planting Movement* which took place in a certain country of Latin America[1] in the 1990s. The total number of churches among the group increased from 129 to 2,600 and the number of baptized believers grew from 7,000 to 19,000 with more than 2,600 annual baptisms. One of the primary factors in this move of God, as is almost always the case with these *Church Planting Movements,* was prayer and intercession. Prayer saturated the lives of these believers who often referred to themselves as a "people on their knees."[2]

Garrison tells of a similar revival among the Gypsies of Spain which produced more than 250,000 followers of Christ. This movement was characterized by all night prayer meetings or "going to the mountain" as the Gypsies would say.[3] Churches which are highly effective and which impact the villages, towns and cities of their spheres of influence understand the power of believing prayer and practice it consistently. Through prayer and intercession they indeed impact the world around them. The vast majority of churches in the world, however, are ordinary churches. Ordinary churches have either not seen the astounding power of prayer and intercession, or else, for whatever reasons, have not committed themselves to it.

Why the Prayerlessness?

With all the amazing answers to prayer God is giving today and which He has given throughout church history, why do God's people and churches pray so little? Why are we often so slow to believe and so slack in our prayer lives? Oswald Chambers reminds us that seven times during Jesus' farewell discourse to His followers He promised to do whatever they asked. Incredible! So why do so many of us struggle in this area? What is it that keeps us from simply taking Jesus at His words and believing what He said? Some time ago I was asking God about the prayerlessness in my own life. Following are a few thoughts about prayer and intercession which came in response to the question:

- The enemy seriously fights God's people in this area because he knows what prayer can do. Scarcely anyone who is involved in leadership escapes this onslaught. We must, however, be careful never to use this as an excuse, because Jesus clearly told us He has given us power over all the power of the enemy (Luke 10:19).

- Prayerlessness is a sin, because it is disobedience to what God has specifically commanded us in His Word (See Matthew 7:7–12; Luke 11:1–13; Luke 18:1–8; Romans 12:12; Ephesians 6:18; Philippians 4:6; 1 Thessalonians 5:17).

- The root of prayerlessness is often slothfulness, unbelief, and selfishness—slothfulness because we often allow the enemy to easily defeat us, sometimes because we are too lazy to fight; unbelief because faith is a choice we make to believe and trust what God has said; and selfishness because so much of our time is consumed on selfish interests and pursuits (television, radio, entertainment, computer games, dawdling away precious time, etc.).

In order to finish *The Great Commission* in this generation, there must be a revival of prayer in churches around the world. So many of God's plans and promises are hanging in the balance, waiting for Jesus' followers to rise up in faith and lay hold of them. *Great*

Commission Churches across the globe are rising to this challenge, diligently teaching and practicing principles of prayer, and motivating their members to powerful intercession. God is indeed answering those prayers as new converts are added, new churches planted, and new people groups reached with the Gospel.

PRACTICAL APPLICATION FOR CHAPTER SIX

1. Think about your own private prayer life. Are you interceding regularly for lost family, friends, and neighbors? Are you praying regularly for the world's unreached peoples? Are you daily asking God to "send more laborers into the harvest?" If not, why not? If you are, how can you more effectively share what is happening in your prayer life with others?

2. What is your church or group doing about prayer and intercession? If it has regular prayer times, think about joining in these vital activities. If they do not, what can you do to spark a prayer movement in your church or city? Ask God for insight into this area.

3. Is there a prayer movement in your country which is uniting to bring down the evil spiritual forces that dominate and rule? If so, please think about joining it. If not, pray about starting one. Perhaps the *Global Day of Prayer* is the place to begin.

4. You can find good help both for personal and public prayer emphases at the following websites:

    www.globaldayofprayer.com

www.win1040.com
www.worldprayerteam.org
www.odusa.org
www.harvestevangelism.org
www.wagnerleadership.org
www.ethne.net
www.global-prayer-digest.com

Endnotes

1 For security reasons Garrison often does not name the particular country and the people group being illustrated.

2 See *Church Planting Movements*, David Garrison, p. 135.

3 Ibid, p.173.

PASSION FOR EVANGELISM

THE THIRD CHARACTERISTIC OF GREAT COMMISSION CHURCHES

"To the weak I became as weak, that I might win the weak. I have become all things to all men, that I might by all means save some."

(1 Corinthians 9:22)

The third characteristic of churches which impact their world is that they have a passion to win lost people to Christ. One of the most needful things for churches all over the world, if they are to genuinely make a difference in their communities and if we are to finish *The Great Commission* in this generation, is for their members to capture the passion for lost people that motivated the life of Jesus.

The Passion of Jesus for Lost People

An interesting verse of Scripture is found in Luke 19:10—a verse which might be called a *mission statement* for Jesus. At the close of His encounter with Zacchaeus,

Jesus revealed the consuming passion of His life when He said, "For the Son of Man is come to seek and to save lost people." It was this zeal for the lost which compelled Jesus to go through Samaria to find the Samaritan woman, which drove Him to the region of the Gadarenes (Gerasenes) to find Legion the demoniac and which caused Him to weep over Jerusalem at their failure to recognize and receive Him. It was this zeal that made Jesus willing to suffer and die on the Cross for lost humanity. The Church of Jesus Christ must understand that the salvation of lost humanity was the reason Jesus came into the world. It was and is and will forever be the primary motivational force in Jesus' life. If we are to effectively do our job as *the Body of Christ* in the world, it must become our passion as well. As this happens—as the hearts of Jesus' followers everywhere are captured by His love for lost humanity—we will be, in the highest sense of the word, Christ's fellow laborers.

Why Passion for Evangelism Is Important

Many years ago Emil Brunner, a German theologian, made the statement: "the church exists by mission [evangelism] as a fire exists by burning." What did he mean? In order to explain, let me ask a question: How much fire can be present if nothing is burning? The answer is, of course, "none at all." If nothing is burning, there can be no fire. Why? Because the very nature of fire is that it burns. Whenever you see something burning, you can always be certain that fire is present—because that's what fire does. Let's take the concept a step further and ask ourselves what Brunner is saying in this statement about the church, God's people. He is saying that unless a church is regularly winning people to Christ, it is not, in reality, a church. It may be a religious organization. It may be a group of people who meet together regularly to worship, pray, and teach God's Word, but Brunner is implying that unless a church is consistently bringing lost men, women, youth, and children into true faith in Jesus Christ, then it is not really a church. Why? Because the *nature* of the church is that it wins people to Christ. Churches are the *Body of Christ.* They do what Jesus did.

Dr. David Shibley expresses this point forcefully when he says, "Any church that is not seriously involved in world evangelism has forfeited its biblical right to exist." What a powerful statement! If this is truly the case, then tens of thousands of churches all over the world have surrendered their right to exist. Evangelist Rheinhard Bonnke says, "The church which does not seek the lost is lost itself." May God help us regain Jesus' passionate heart to reach lost people! And He is indeed helping us to do just that. In my travels around the world, I am finding more and more churches, especially in the Two-Thirds World, who are zealous about reaching people for Christ—and who, I might add, are becoming experts at the task. These churches are helping tens of thousands of people come to faith in Christ and are planting thousands of churches throughout their countries because the passion of Jesus is in them as well.

Examples of Passion for Evangelism

Three examples of passion for evangelism will illustrate the point. The first is the Apostle Paul. There is an amazing passage in Romans 9:1–4 that has often not been understood clearly. Listen to Paul's words, "I tell the truth in Christ, I am not lying, my conscience also bearing me witness in the Holy Spirit, that I have great sorrow and continual grief in my heart. For I could wish that I myself were accursed from Christ for my brethren, my countrymen according to the flesh." Do you grasp what Paul is saying here? First, he describes himself as having "great sorrow and continual grief." What is he talking about? He is talking about his burden for the people of Israel to come to Christ. Oh that more of Christ's followers today would gain this kind of burden! But the next statement is almost incomprehensible. Paul says that his burden for Israel's salvation is such that he would be willing to pay *any* price for them to come to Christ. In fact, Paul is saying that he would be willing to pay the *ultimate* price for his people to be saved. Please understand clearly. Paul is declaring here that, if it would help Israel to come to know Christ, he would be willing to go to hell in their place! That's what it means to be "accursed from Christ." When I read that record, my mouth drops open. It is almost more than I can grasp. How could anyone have that kind of passion for lost people? With that kind of zeal, is it any wonder that Paul was so instrumental in impacting cities, countries, and continents for Christ?

A second example of passion for evangelism is John Knox, a man who, to a considerable extent, impacted an entire country for Christ. Living in Scotland in the sixteenth century, John Knox's life affected nearly every segment of Scottish society. One of history's notable national revivals came to Scotland largely because of this man. Thousands of Scots came to faith in Christ through the influence of John Knox. Hundreds of churches were formed through his impact. A significant part of the nation was converted through His efforts. Few men have affected a country so deeply. How did that happen? How can the life of one man influence an entire country? I do not wish to be simplistic here, but much of the answer to that question is found in one of Knox's most famous sayings. That saying is in reality a prayer—a passionate prayer: "Give me Scotland or I die!" Do you sense the spiritual fervor in that prayer? Can you hear the passion? One reason John Knox was so instrumental in helping to bring revival to Scotland is because of the passion that was in his heart. And do you know what happened as a result of this passionate cry? God gave him Scotland!

May God give us more pastors, evangelists, missionaries, church planters, leaders, and intercessors with a passion like this man's. What a difference it would make in the world if *you* were able to gain a zeal for your community like John Knox did for Scotland: "Give me my city (town, village, people group) or I die!" This is one way societies are transformed.

The life of missionary-statesman J. Hudson Taylor offers a similar example of the passion I am attempting to describe. He is another man who significantly influenced a country. Many will agree that the amazing revival going on presently in China is possible because of the efforts of people like Hudson Taylor who laid a solid foundation for the Church of Jesus Christ there. At one point Taylor's *China Inland Mission* had nearly 1,000 zealous missionaries across China who were willing to suffer almost any hardship and who were even willing to die for the Gospel. In fact, in those days one was required to sign a commitment that he was indeed willing to die for China before the organization would accept him as a missionary. Some of these missionaries carried their belongings to China in a casket because of the certainty that they would not return to their homelands. The same was true of missionaries in other countries and on other continents. But how did this happen? How does one build a missionary organization like *China Inland Mission?* Here again, a part of the answer is found in one of Hudson Taylor's most famous quotations: "I felt that I could not go on living unless I did something for China!" Statements like this reveal the zeal for the lost people of China that was in Taylor's heart—and which must be in ours if we are to make significant impact on our communities.

These are three excellent examples of people who had a passion for evangelism that was so profound that it shook entire countries. Passion enables ordinary people to do extraordinary things. I believe each of these three men were, in many ways, ordinary men. They were not born in nobility and wealth. They were common men with an uncommon fervor to win people to Christ and to shake countries in the process.

How to Gain a Heart for Evangelism

This uncommon zeal for lost people is one of the qualities which must be regained if we are to finish *The Great Commission* in this generation. How does it come to a congregation? How does this passion for souls get into the heart of a church or an organization? The answer lies with the pastor or the primary leader of the group. He is the only one who can inspire it. If such passion is in him, it can get into the heart of the body. If it is not in him, it will almost never become characteristic of his church or group. But if this passion for the lost is indeed in him, how does he transfer it to the church? It is conveyed from the primary leader to the church membership in the following ways:

- By preaching consistently and fervently about evangelism. One of the reasons some congregations do not have a deep burden for lost people is that their leaders do not preach and teach about it on a regular basis— and because, when they do so, it is often without conviction and zeal.

- By demonstrating passion for evangelism in his own life. A burden for the lost *must* be modeled by the senior leadership of the group. The church members need to see it in every aspect of the pastor's life. He should be winning more people to Christ than anyone in the church. The people must see him not only preaching about this need, but must also see him weeping and praying over the lost and practically involved in reaching them.

- By honoring people in the congregation who are effectively reaching lost people. Whatever qualities come to be *characteristic* of a church will be largely determined by the qualities which are honored in the life of that body by its leadership. If a church is to gain a passion for souls, then the senior leadership must find a way to esteem and honor members who are effective in evangelism.

- By spending church money on evangelism. One of the primary things which reflect the true values of any person or organization is how their money is spent. If we say we value something, but do not spend money on it, we likely are deceiving ourselves. One of the largest items in any church's budget, if the church is to have a genuine passion for lost people—and if it is to be effective in reaching the unsaved—should be evangelism and missions. If we want to win people to Christ, we must, as we say, "put our money where our mouth is."

- By teaching the people to consistently pray for unsaved family, friends, and neighbors. This prayer emphasis is vital in any church or organization if they are to develop vision and passion for evangelism and church planting.

Four Keys to Effective Evangelism

As we examine this third characteristic of *Great Commission Churches*, it is important to take a look at some ways to evangelize more effectively. I want to share four of the most successful methods of evangelism in the world today. The majority of the people who are won to Christ, in every country of the world, are won in one of the following ways:

The first key is to help church members seriously focus in prayer on lost family, friends, and neighbors. An effective way to do this is for each person in the congregation to develop an *Evangelistic Prayer List*. Allow me to explain by giving you an assignment—one which has two parts. The first part of your assignment is to list on a piece of paper the name of every person you know who does not have a personal relationship with Christ. Begin by thinking about your family and relatives. Then reflect on your friends. Next think about your neighbors—those who live around you. Then consider people with whom you do business. Write down the name of every person you know who is not born again. (A form for helping you do this is included in the *Resources* section at the close of this book.)

The second part of the assignment is to think carefully and prayerfully through your list of names. On a separate and smaller piece of paper, please write the names of the ten people (from your big list) who are, in your opinion, most open to hearing about Jesus right now. Begin with the first name on your list. Ask yourself, "Is this person open to my telling him about Christ right now?" If the answer is "yes," write his name on the smaller piece of paper. If "no," go to the second name. At the top of this second and smaller piece of paper, write: "My Evangelistic Prayer List." Your goal is to go through all the names on your big list until you have ten names written on your *Evangelistic Prayer List*. (A form to help you make an *Evangelistic Prayer List* is included in the *Resources* section at the close of this book.)

Once you have created this list, put it in your Bible and begin praying for these ten people every day during your devotional period. Ask the Holy Spirit to convict them, to draw them to Jesus, and to give them a personal revelation of who He is. Next, look for opportunities to talk to these people about Christ and to invite them to a Gospel meeting. It is vital to understand that *the most effective form of evangelism in the entire world is inviting people to a church meeting or to a Gospel crusade.* Research consistently shows that between seventy and ninety percent of all the people who give their lives to Christ do so because a friend or relative invites them to church or to a Gospel meeting. Isn't that amazing? The most effective form of evangelism available to man costs no money and can be done by almost anyone.

Permit me a personal testimony. I was converted to Christ during my final year of secondary school. A few months later I left home for my university studies. I was a new believer and did not know how to properly witness to unsaved people. At university I met a friend who did not know Christ. Regularly I prayed for this friend. During a series of Gospel meetings at the church I was attending, I asked my friend if he would go with me to church. To my surprise he agreed and that night my friend surrendered his life to Christ. He went back with me the next night and was baptized in the Holy Spirit. Again, the third night he went with me to the Gospel services and received a specific call from God to Christian ministry. During those three days he also met the woman who was to become his wife. For the past forty years my friend has preached the Gospel all over the USA, winning many people to Christ. At the time of this writing, he is serving as president of a Christian university in the USA where he is training scores of young people to be pastors, evangelists, and missionaries for Christ. All of this happened because a young teenager—a new convert—simply invited a friend to a Gospel meeting.

Once you have finished your *Evangelistic Prayer*

List, it will be important to begin teaching other believers in your church or group to do likewise. If a pastor or leader will do this one simple thing, it will help to focus his entire congregation on evangelism. If there are twenty members in a church or group, this exercise will also immediately give the congregation 200 outstanding new prospects for evangelism. If the church or group has 100 members, it will instantly give 1,000 new good prospects. If they have 1,000 it will result in 10,000 quality prospects. *Please do not underestimate the significance of this assignment.* Keep in mind that one thing which has always caused the Body of Christ to thrive in the societies of the world is the passing of the Gospel from individual to individual, family to family, friend to friend, and village to village.

A second effective means of evangelism is to reach out to people who are experiencing a crisis in their lives. Please remember that people are most open to the Gospel when they are in a crisis situation of some kind. Look at the people Jesus ministered to: Mary Magdalene, Bartimaeus, the Leper, Legion the demoniac, the woman of Samaria, the woman with the cancerous issue of blood, the Roman Centurion. The list could go on. The people whose lives Jesus touched were often in the midst of tragedy and adversity.

In every part of the world people can be found who have no interest in hearing about Jesus—until tragedy strikes their family. A dear friend of mine in India was reared as a caste Hindu. He hated Jesus and His followers and, by his own admission, used to throw rocks at them when they passed near his home. He was also a member of a militant Hindu political party in India. However, everything changed one day when the doctors told him that his wife had an incurable heart condition and was going to die. Suddenly he became interested in the prayers of believers. A friend invited his wife to a Gospel Healing Crusade. That night this man's wife was both converted and healed of the heart condition. Today his entire family is serving Christ with their whole hearts. His daughter and son-in-law are working among unreached villages of India. Why? Because someone reached out to them during a time of family crisis and invited them to a Gospel meeting. One simple and effective means of evangelism is to teach people to look around for friends and neighbors who are experiencing major problems and to reach out to them with the love and compassion of Jesus.

The third key to effective evangelism is ministry to children and youth. One study in the USA found that 43% of all followers of Jesus began their walk with Him before the age of thirteen. Sixty-four percent began their walk with Christ before the age of eighteen. Similar statistics have been found in other countries. It is simply a fact that most people begin following Christ while they are young—before their hearts have had a chance to harden. If we want to be effective at evangelism, we need to remember this. Children's Crusades, Christian schools, Sunday School, Vacation Bible School, and similar activities are extremely valuable in reaching youth for Christ. It is important also to teach children and youth to make an *Evangelistic Prayer List* in order to help develop in them a heart for evangelism at an early age and to help them reach family and friends for Christ.

A fourth key to effective evangelism is the *Jesus Film*. Although there are many excellent evangelistic tools available today, the *Jesus Film* deserves to be singled out. Without question this is the most effective evangelism instrument in history. The film has now received more than six billion viewings[1] and is available, at the time of this writing, in 947 different languages. Translation into another 209 languages is in process at the moment. Incredibly, approximately 201 million people, including some of the world's least-reached peoples, have indicated decisions to accept Jesus Christ as personal Savior and Lord through this film. Many churches and organizations are finding the *Jesus Film* to be one of their most successful methods of evangelism and church planting.

These four forms of evangelism, if done with excellence, consistency, wisdom, and passion, will help a church become much more effective at reaching lost people. Churches which impact the world understand and practice these things. *Great Commission Churches* are passionate about winning people to Christ.

The Essence of the Gospel

Before leaving the subject of evangelism, it is important to review just what the Gospel of Jesus Christ is—to insure we are communicating precisely and biblically with unbelievers. What is a believer in Christ? What does it mean to be a true follower of Jesus? What is the "good news" about Jesus Christ that we are to share with others? All of these are important questions and it is vital to answer them with clarity if we are to be faithful servants and if we are to see people come to genuine faith in Christ.

Let's begin with an understanding of evangelism. In paragraph four of *The Lausanne Covenant*[2], the task of evangelism is defined as follows: "To evangelize is to spread the good news that Jesus Christ died for our sins and was raised from the dead according to the Scriptures, and that as the reigning Lord he now offers the forgiveness of sins and the liberating gift of the Spirit to all who believe." This statement, along with others like it, implies that to be a true follower of Jesus involves two issues: 1) a person's sins must be forgiven, and 2) the control of his life must be surrendered to the reigning Lord.

Coming to Christ involves, first of all, getting rid of our sins, so that we can have a real relationship with the living God through Jesus Christ. The Bible clearly states that "all of us have sinned and fall short of the glory of God" (Romans 3:23). How true. We are also reminded that these sins have separated us from God (Isaiah 59:1–2). Our sins are like a wall between us and a holy God which keeps us from relationship with Him. When a person puts his faith in Jesus Christ, he acknowledges that Jesus alone, because of His suffering, death and resurrection, can wash away our sins and enable us to enter into meaningful relationship with the Creator (Acts 4:12; John 10:7–10 1 Corinthians 15:12–15). The wall which had separated us from God comes down and we are able to enter into dynamic fellowship with the living God. This is what the Bible refers to as *eternal life* (John 17:3). In Scripture eternal life is not only about living forever in Heaven, but also about knowing God and having His life within here and now. The Scriptures say that when our sins are forgiven, they are forgiven *forever* and are *forgotten* by God, never to be remembered against us again (Acts 2:38; Psalm 103:12; Isaiah 43:25).

The second aspect of becoming a follower of Jesus has to do with Lordship—who is going to be God of our lives. True conversion involves the genuine surrender of the *control* of one's life to Christ and the forsaking of all other gods. From the moment a person becomes a true believer, his primary purpose in life will be to follow Christ and obey Him in everything. How we talk, how we think, how we treat other people, who we marry, what we do for a life-occupation—everything in life is affected by that decision. Jesus becomes Lord of all. At the moment of faith and submission, one becomes a son or daughter of the living God and begins a life of walking and talking with God. At that point he receives the liberating gift of the Spirit and no longer lives a self-centered life. Each new believer is supernaturally enabled to live for Christ and others. He is born again.

When we preach, teach, or talk to people about becoming followers of Jesus, it is important to help them understand these two issues which, when effectively dealt with, result in conversion. It is also important to help them understand that salvation cannot be earned. It comes totally by grace and is a *gift* from God (Ephesians 2:8–9; Romans 3:21–24). The essence of the "good news" is that Jesus took the punishment for my sins on the cross and, because of His vicarious death and resurrection, I can be forgiven and have a personal relationship with the true and living God.

The primary point of this chapter is that churches which make a genuine difference in the world are passionate about getting the message of Jesus and His love to family, friends, and neighbors who do not know Him. These churches have the heart of Jesus to "seek and save lost people." Churches which are not regularly winning people to Christ probably do not want to win them badly enough. True love will always find a way.

PRACTICAL APPLICATION FOR CHAPTER SEVEN:

1. Think about David Shibley's statement: "Any church that is not seriously involved in world evangelism has forfeited its biblical right to exist." How does this statement apply to your church? Is your church or group seriously involved in spreading the Gospel around the world? If not, why not? If so, what is the most effective way you are winning people to Christ?

2. Think about how you can begin to build a passion for evangelism in your church or organization. Read the part of this chapter again which deals with "How to Build a Heart for Evangelism." Which of these things do you need to emphasize to help build this passion in the people of your church or group?

3. Please take the time now to do the exercise on making an *Evangelistic Prayer List.* Read that part of the chapter again and make your two lists. Once you have

made your smaller list, put it in your Bible and begin praying for your ten relatives or friends on a daily basis. Look for opportunities to speak to them about Christ or to invite them to one of your church gatherings or to a Gospel meeting. It could change their lives forever.

4. Think about some unsaved people you know who are currently experiencing a crisis in their lives. What can you do to reach out to them with the love of Jesus?

ENDNOTES

1   Obviously six billion different individuals have not seen the *Jesus Film* since nearly two billion have yet to hear the Gospel for the first time. Many people have viewed the film multiple times.

2   The Lausanne Covenant is a declaration agreed upon by more than 2,300 evangelicals during the 1974 International Congress in Lausanne, Switzerland, to be more intentional about world evangelization. Since then, the Covenant has challenged churches and Christian organizations to work together to make Jesus Christ known throughout the world.

MINISTERING WITH SUPERNATURAL POWER

THE FOURTH CHARACTERISTIC OF GREAT COMMISSION CHURCHES

"The Spirit of the Lord is upon Me, because He has anointed Me to preach the gospel to the poor; He has sent Me to heal the brokenhearted, to proclaim liberty to the captives and recovery of sight to the blind, to set at liberty those who are oppressed; to proclaim the acceptable year of the Lord."

(Luke 4:18–19)

The fourth characteristic of churches which impact their worlds is that they minister in their communities with supernatural power. I want to remind us of an important truth—the Great Commission was given to us in the context of *power*. Earlier I referenced that *The Great Commission* was repeated in some form at least five times in the New Testament. One of those places is Mark 16:15–18 where Mark quotes Jesus' words as follows:

And He said to them, "Go into all the world and preach the gospel to every creature. He who believes and is baptized will be saved; but he who does not believe will be condemned. And these signs will follow those who believe: In My name they will cast out demons; they will speak with new tongues; they will take up serpents; and if they drink anything deadly, it will by no means hurt them; they will lay hands on the sick, and they will recover."

Many are aware of the debate over whether Mark 16:9–20 actually belongs in the New Testament record, since two of the reliable early manuscripts do not include it. However, two things are not debatable about this matter. First, the passage is included in almost every translation of Scripture, even if it is footnoted in some way. Almost every published version of the Bible has embraced it in the biblical record in some form. That is significant. The second factor of note is that this passage harmonizes with the rest of Scripture. No new truth is introduced and nothing is said that is not confirmed by numerous other biblical passages. (See Matthew 8:28–34; Matthew 9:35; Luke 9:1–6; Luke 10:1–20; Acts 3:1–10; Acts 5:12–16; Acts 9:32–35; Acts 16:16–18; Romans 15:17–22; 1 Corinthians 12:27–31.)

The Power of the Holy Spirit

In an earlier chapter I referenced Acts 1:8, which highlights an important point. In that verse, according to Jesus, the primary purpose of the baptism (infilling, anointing, clothing, empowering—whatever one wishes to call it) of the Holy Spirit is to enable us to be effective witnesses for Him throughout the earth. We must understand there was a reason why Jesus *commanded* His disciples not to leave Jerusalem until they received this empowering. Jesus knew the infilling of the Spirit would be essential for the disciples to effectively carry out the work of *The Great Commission,* because that work, in order to be most effective, would require the supernatural power of the Holy Spirit.

The Coming of the Kingdom

It is interesting to note that, as Jesus began His ministry, the first words out of His mouth were, "Repent, for the kingdom of heaven is at hand" (Matthew 4:17). What did He mean by saying the Kingdom was now *at hand?* The expression literally means "within one's grasp." Jesus was saying to the people, because He (the Messiah King) was now present in the world, the benefits of His Kingdom were now close enough that people could lay hold of them. These Kingdom benefits were now within the reach of ordinary people. This was a revolutionary message. For generations the people of Israel had heard that one day, when Messiah appeared, He would bring the glory of God's Kingdom with Him. The Kingdom Age would be a time of unprecedented blessing—of peace, joy, justice, deliverance, prosperity, and wholeness. In His preaching Jesus was saying that He, the Messiah, was indeed now present in the world and that He was bringing with Him the blessings of God's Kingdom. What good news! Matthew goes on to say,

> And Jesus went about all Galilee, teaching in their synagogues, preaching the gospel of the kingdom, and

healing all kinds of sickness and all kinds of disease among the people. Then His fame went throughout all Syria; and they brought to Him all sick people who were afflicted with various diseases and torments, and those who were demon-possessed, epileptics, and paralytics; and He healed them.

(Matthew 4:23–24)

It is apparent from this record, along with numerous similar passages, that Jesus not only *preached* to the people that the Kingdom was now present (albeit in infancy),[1] but also *demonstrated* that truth. He did so in two ways: by healing sick people and casting out evil spirits. Later, Jesus stated, "And if I cast out demons by the Spirit of God, surely the kingdom of God has come upon you" (Matthew 12:28). As these two things happened, Jesus said the people would know convincingly that the much-anticipated *Kingdom of God* was indeed present among them and within their grasp. George Eldon Ladd affirms Jesus' teaching was intended to show people how they might enter God's Kingdom and that His miracles were intended to prove the Kingdom of God had indeed come to them.

Interestingly, when Jesus began sending out His followers in ministry, He did so with the instructions that they should minister to people in the same ways He had done. They also should preach the good news of the Kingdom and demonstrate its presence among the people by healing the sick and casting out evil spirits. Here is Luke's account of the sending out of the Twelve: "Then He called His twelve disciples together and gave them power and authority over all demons, and to cure diseases. He sent them to preach the kingdom of God and to heal the sick" (Luke 9:1–2). Following those instructions, the record says, "So they departed and went throughout the towns, preaching the gospel and healing the sick everywhere" (Luke 9:6).

Lest we think this kind of ministry was intended only for the Twelve, similar directives were given to the seventy others who were trained and sent out by Jesus. Listen to Luke's report of their commissioning:

> After these things the Lord appointed seventy[2] others also, and sent them two by two before His face into every city and place where He himself was about to go..."Whatever city you enter, and they receive you, eat such things as are set before you. And heal the sick there, and say to them, 'The kingdom of God has come near to you.'"
>
> (Luke 10:1,8–9)

The instructions, together with the expectations, were nearly identical for both the Twelve and the Seventy. It is clear Jesus wanted His followers to tell the people the Kingdom of God was present among them (within their grasp) and to confirm the truth of the statement by ministering with supernatural power (healing the sick and casting out evil spirits) in order for people who were held captive by Satan to be set free.

The Spread of the Kingdom

As one honestly examines the biblical record, it is also clear that Jesus never intended supernatural ministry to people, which characterized His preaching and teaching, to end. Look at what He said in John 14: "Most assuredly, I say to you, he who believes in Me, the works that I do he will do also..." (v. 12a). There is no indication here (or elsewhere) that these works were to end with the Apostles. In fact, the opposite is clearly stated. Jesus declared these works will be done by "he who believes in Me." He goes on to say, "...and greater works than these he will do, because I go to My Father" (v. 12b). Jesus continues, "And whatever you ask in My name, that I will do, that the Father may be glorified in the Son. If you ask anything in My name, I will do it" (vv. 13–14).

All over the world people are taking Jesus at His word and seeing God move with power and authority through their own ministries. Estimates indicate that 70% of all conversions taking place in the world today are the result of signs and wonders. In fact, one study done in India showed that 81% of all Hindus who became Christians did so because of some miracle God worked in their lives or in the lives of family members.

If *The Great Commission* is to be completed in this generation, there are three great religious worlds which must be reached: the worlds of Islam, Hinduism, and Buddhism. The most effective way to penetrate these enormous religious systems is through God's love and supernatural power. As I travel throughout the Two-Thirds World, over and over I hear testimonies of God's love for people demonstrated in signs and wonders. Here is one of hundreds of examples. This testimony comes from a national missionary in the country of Laos:

God has been using illness to bring people to Himself. In the past few months, we've had many people show interest in the things of God because they were suffering from a physical ailment. Many unsaved Laotians who couldn't be helped by doctors or hospitals have turned to our churches for healing prayers. God has shown His power by healing many.[3]

Miracles like these are happening in the world on a daily basis, especially in the nations of the Majority World—and they are happening through the lives of both ministers and laymen.

One of my friends who lives and works in a Muslim country tells how his family came to Christ. When he was a young man, his mother became demonized. The demonic oppression resulted in her loss of speech. For several months she was unable to communicate except through the writing of notes. The condition progressed and developed into paralysis in her right arm, leaving the family perplexed and confused. About this time my friend heard of a national evangelist who was working in his country. People said this man could heal sick people. My friend, not knowing what else to do, went to find this evangelist. He convinced him to come to his home and pray for his mother. The evangelist came, laid his hands on her, and took authority over the evil spirit in the name of Jesus. Instantly my friend's mother was set free and healed both of her dumbness and the paralysis in her arm. As a result, the entire family came to Christ and is actively ministering in their country today.

All over the world supernatural miracles like this

woman's deliverance are happening. Hindus, Muslims, and Buddhists who have no interest in becoming followers of Jesus, are developing genuine interest in the prayers of believers (or anyone else for that matter) when doctors tell them a wife or mother or child has cancer and is going to die. When faced with a major crisis, things change. People rapidly develop interest in anything which offers them hope.

Paul's Church Planting Strategy

It is interesting to note the primary strategy which Paul seems to have used in church planting was this very thing—believing God to demonstrate His love and power by healing sick people and seeing them set free from Satan's bondage. Here is Paul's own testimony:

> For I will not dare to speak of any of those things which Christ has accomplished through me, in word and deed, to make the Gentiles obedient—in mighty signs and wonders, by the power of the Spirit of God, so that from Jerusalem and round about to Illyricum I have fully preached the gospel of Christ.
>
> (Romans 15:18–19)

Paul understood the difficulty of penetrating strongholds of the enemy. He knew this could be done most effectively through the demonstration of God's supernatural power. To the Corinthians Paul wrote, "Truly the signs of an apostle were accomplished among you with all perseverance, in signs and wonders and mighty deeds" (2 Corinthians 12:12).

Roland Allen, in his classic book *Missionary Methods—St. Paul's or Ours,* reminds us in the Acts of the Apostles, Luke speaks of miracles in Paul's life as if they were a natural and appropriate part of his ministry. Allen says the use of miracles in Paul's ministry, although they were not used as an enticement to people to receive his teaching, certainly did help him in the following four ways:[4]

- The miracles attracted hearers.

- The miracles helped affirm Paul's authenticity in the minds of people who heard him.

- The miracles were illustrations of the character of the gospel Paul was preaching (love, compassion for the weak, release from bondage, etc.).

- The miracles illustrated the release of God's salvation to the poor, the weak, and the suffering.

God Heals the Unsaved

Like Paul, churches which impact their worlds and demonstrate God's Kingdom understand the importance of the miraculous. In simple faith, they take God at His word. These churches do not rationalize, spiritualize, or explain away the truths Jesus proclaimed. They believe God will do what He said He would do. As a result, they regularly reap the rewards of simple faith as people for whom they pray experience God's power and regularly surrender their lives to Christ.

Great Commission Churches believe God loves people and He still delights to show His love by bringing wholeness into their lives. They understand God loves to heal *unsaved* people. Look at the biblical record.

The vast majority of people who were healed by Christ and His followers were not Christ-followers *before* they were cured. There was no requirement—no condition that God placed on them—to make a commitment to Him before they were healed. In fact, it was often the actual demonstration of God's love and power in their lives that got their attention and made them *want* to be followers of Jesus, the Messiah. Everywhere I travel in the Two-Thirds World, I hear similar reports of people coming to Christ because of miracles God has worked in their lives or in the lives of family members. David Garrison tells of a researcher who recently returned from the state of Bihar in India with this testimony: "I interviewed about 50 believers. Every one of them knew Jesus as healer before they knew Him as Savior."[5]

A Practical Idea

With this in mind, let me share an idea. Drs. Paul Gupta and Sherwood Lingengenfelter, in their book *Breaking Tradition to Accomplish Vision* (BMH Books, Winona Lake, IN), believe that every local church should have a team of evangelists which is regularly engaged in praying for sick people, ministering to those in need, and proclaiming the good news of the Kingdom in their communities, especially to the unconverted. Gupta contends this is not simply work that should be done in evangelistic campaigns and gospel healing crusades. Rather it should be the daily work of the church. I agree.

Being Used in the Supernatural

Perhaps you are wondering how you might personally be

used by God to see His supernatural power demonstrated in the lives of people around you in order for more of them to come to Christ. There are at least three keys for the release of God's supernatural power in our lives:

The first principle is *being filled with the Holy Spirit.* I am aware this has been a matter of some controversy in the Body of Christ. However, most of God's people around the world agree on the following issues in this discussion:

- Everyone needs the Holy Spirit in life and ministry. Otherwise Jesus would not have commanded His followers to remain in Jerusalem until they had received this "baptism with the Holy Spirit" (Acts 1:5–8) and Paul never would have commanded his converts to "be filled with the Spirit" (Ephesians 5:18). The fullness of the Spirit is, in the biblical record, vital for effective witness and service.

- The infilling of the Spirit happens more than once. The record of Acts is that Jesus' followers were filled again and again with the Holy Spirit (See Acts 2:4; 4:8; 4:31; 7:55; 11:24; 13:9; 13:52). Sometimes the text says they were filled with the Spirit and sometimes it says they were full of the Spirit, and often it is speaking of some of the same people who were filled with the Spirit on different occasions. A story is told of the great evangelist D. L. Moody who often spoke of the need for regular infilling of the Spirit in a person's life. When asked why he needed to be filled with the Spirit over and over, Moody replied, "Because I leak!" Most of us do. We are filled with the Holy Spirit (and faith, vision, passion and anointing) but some-how, in the hard work of life and ministry, the sense of the Spirit's power seeps out and needs to be renewed.

- The infilling of the Spirit comes from God. It is not something which one works up in his own psyche. It is one of God's many gifts to His children.

- The baptism of power is a work of grace. We do not earn it or deserve it. God gives this infilling because He loves us, because we need it in order to be effective in ministry for Him, and because we ask for it.

Truly effective ministry requires that God's people be filled with the Spirit. As believers are filled with and empowered for service by the Holy Spirit, God often opens to them a new door into the realm of the su-pernatural. Following this experience with God, they often receive new faith, new boldness, and new abil-ity to pray for sick people and see them get well. This has happened over and over in the lives of believers throughout the centuries. It is what Jesus said would happen.

The second principle is *cultivating intimacy of relation-ship with Jesus.* Each of Christ's followers who desire to be used of Him must understand that power and au-thority tend to flow from intimacy with God. People who are used of God in supernatural ways are normally those who walk closely with God, who draw near to Him, and who are intent on listening to the voice of the Spirit. Andrew Murray reminds us that being alone with God "is the secret of true prayer, of true power in prayer, of real living, of face-to-face fellowship with

God, and of power for service." Murray adds, "There is no true, deep conversion; no true, deep holiness; no clothing with the Holy Spirit and with power; no abiding peace or joy, without being daily alone with God."[6] Pastor David Yonggi Cho, who serves as Senior Pastor for the world's largest church, reminds us that being filled with the Holy Spirit is normally in direct proportion to our prayer lives. According to Pastor Cho, there is no way a person can be full of the Spirit without prayer.

Many years ago, one of God's special servants in England who was powerfully used in the supernatural was asked the secret of his success. His reply was, "I live with me ear cocked to heaven." This man understood the importance of intimacy and of knowing the mind of the Spirit. On one occasion Jesus said, "...the sheep hear his voice [the voice of the Shepherd]; and he calls his own sheep by name and leads them out. And when he brings out his own sheep, he goes before them; and the sheep follow him, for they know his voice" (John 10:3–4). Certainly this was one reason Jesus was so effective in ministry. In John 5, Jesus reminded His followers, "Most assuredly, I say to you, the Son can do nothing of Himself, but what He sees the Father do; for whatever He does, the Son also does in like manner. For the Father loves the Son, and shows Him all things that He Himself does..." (John 5:19–20). Jesus' intimacy of relationship with the Father, which included His ability to know the Father's voice, was significant to His effectiveness.

People who develop deep intimacy with God are those who spend regular, daily time alone with God in prayer, and who periodically get away for special seasons of fasting. For ages, fasting and prayer have been essential to the powerful anointing of the Spirit in peoples' lives. In the Bible the discipline of fasting was practiced by Moses, David, Elijah, Ezra, Daniel, Jesus, Paul, and many others. In modern history people such as Martin Luther, John Calvin, John Wesley, John Knox, Jonathan Edwards and Charles Finney discovered new intimacy with God through fasting and prayer. A number of years ago, Dr. Bill Bright, founder of *Campus Crusade for Christ,* made this comment about prayer and fasting: "He [God] has shown me the most powerful way to evangelize the world is to bring men and women to this biblical discipline [of fasting], which enables them to develop an intimate love relationship with Christ and motivates them to win others to Christ."

The biblical account of the inability of Jesus' disciples to cast the unclean spirit out of the tormented child is a case in point (Mark 9:14–29). In response to the disciples' question concerning why they were unable to cast the dumb spirit out of the boy, Jesus replied, "This kind can come out by nothing but prayer and fasting."[7] Jesus knew and taught the need of these disciplines in the lives of His followers, if they were to be effective in ministry.

Isaiah 58 is perhaps the greatest treatise God has given in all of Scripture on fasting. Here God reminds us the power of true fasting (with right motives) is to..."loose the bonds of wickedness, to undo the heavy burdens, to let the oppressed go free, and that you break every yoke" (Isaiah 58:6).

The third principle for supernatural ministry is *compassion for people who are suffering.* Compassion is like a magnet which attracts the love and power of God toward hurting people. Over and over in Scripture, when Jesus healed the multitudes, the record says He was "moved with compassion" (Matthew 9:36; Matthew 14:14; Matthew 15:32; Matthew 20:34; Mark 1:41, etc.). It may well have been His deep concern for the misfortune of others which drew Jesus to the multitudes of sick people and which somehow pulled out of Him (or made Him an effective conduit for) the power of God to make these people whole.

This is often true also of God's servants today. A couple of years ago I was in the state of Punjab, India, where I met a simple village pastor, a converted Sikh. He pointed to a young child in his congregation and told me an amazing story. The child's parents, who were Sikhs, came to him to request prayer. For years they had wanted to have a child but the wife remained barren. My pastor friend told the couple that he would be delighted to pray for them because he served a God who loves children. He laid his hands on the couple and asked God, in Jesus' name, to give them a child. About one year later, a beautiful baby boy was born to this couple. For months they rejoiced over their son, but when the child was fourteen months old, he developed a serious lung disease and died. The parents were, of course, heartbroken. The couple took their dead son in their arms and walked across the village to find the pastor who had prayed for them. When they found the pastor, they dumped the motionless child in his arms and asked him this question: "Is that the kind of God you serve—one who gives children to parents and then takes them back?"

The pastor told me that he did not know what to do or say to the parents. He was speechless. The parents turned and walked away, leaving the pastor holding their lifeless son. At that moment, the pastor said, he did not even know how to pray. The only prayer that would come out of his lips was this: "Father, this pain is more than I can bear!" Tears ran down his cheeks as he wondered what to do. But when those tears of compassion dropped on the dead child in his arms, God raised the child from the dead! The child gasped and began crying for his parents. It is quite an understatement to say the pastor was overjoyed. He quickly called out to the child's parents and put their living son back in their arms. "This," he said, "is the kind of God I serve!"[8]

This story illustrates that deep compassion is often crucial to people being used of God in the supernatural. This was true of Jesus and it is true of us. If we want to be effective in ministering to people the life and wholeness that Jesus came to bring, we must humble ourselves and ask God to fill us with His compassion.

The Supernatural and Church Planting Movements

In his book *Church Planting Movements,* David Garrison relates numerous examples of signs and wonders as a regular part of *Church Planting Movements* in many countries of the world. He observes that these *Church Planting Movements* are almost always born and fostered in an atmosphere of God's supernatural manifestations. Garrison tells of an American missionary to China who was unaccustomed to seeing signs and wonders. After a few years of seeing the powerful working of the Holy Spirit in that country, the missionary confessed: "All of the *Church Planting Movements* I have seen in China are full of healings, miracles, and even resurrections."[9]

If you desire to be more effective in ministering God's supernatural power to suffering humanity, think about the three principles just discussed. First, ask God to fill you again with His Holy Spirit. Get alone with Him, wait on Him, and open your heart to Him. Second, make a point to draw nearer to God. Spend regular, private time with Him in prayer. Set aside some days for fasting. Listen for God's voice and walk in obedience to what He is saying. Third, seek God for deep compassion for people who are in distress. Remember that people and churches who impact society are commonly people who minister in supernatural power.

Practical Application for Chapter Eight

1. Spend time meditating on this chapter. Think about how often God uses you to minister His love and power to broken people. Would you like to be used more in this area?

2. Think about people you know (especially unbelievers) who are in need of God's healing or delivering power. Write their names down and begin praying for them in your devotional times. Ask God if He wants you to personally go and pray for them for healing and deliverance.

3. Plan some time to get alone with God for fasting and

prayer. During that time, ask God to fill you again with the power of His Spirit. Ask Him to help you draw near to Him—to be able to hear His voice more clearly. Ask Him to fill you with a deeper compassion for people.

Endnotes

1 John R. W. Stott, noted biblical scholar, reminds us that God's Kingdom is both "now" and "not yet." By that he means it is indeed present in some way and its benefits are available now to mankind, but the full extent of those blessings are to be released at some future date when the King returns to the earth and officially sets up His Kingdom.

2 Some translations read "seventy-two."

3 *Christian Aid E-mail Bulletin*, November, 2004.

4 *Missionary Methods—St. Paul's or Ours*, Wm. B. Eerdmans, Grand Rapids, 1962, pp. 42-47.

5 *Church Planting Movements*, David Garrison, p. 232-233.

6 Andrew Murray: *God's Best Secrets*. Whitaker House, p. 90

7 Some texts omit the words "and fasting."

8 This story was confirmed in a personal interview with this pastor's supervisor.

9 *Church Planting Movements*, David Garrison, p. 233.

EFFECTIVELY DISCIPLING NEW CONVERTS

THE FIFTH CHARACTERISTIC OF GREAT COMMISSION CHURCHES

"Go therefore and make disciples of all the nations...."
(Matthew 28:19)

The fifth characteristic of churches which impact their worlds is that they are proficient in discipling new converts. If we are to make real progress in building churches which are powerful, effective, and impacting on society, it is imperative to understand that the *essence* of Jesus' command in *The Great Commission* is to *make disciples,* not just to win people to Christ or to see them baptized. The word *disciple* in the New Testament means primarily "a learner; a pupil"—one who sits at the feet of a master or teacher in order to learn from him. The implication is that a disciple of someone is a "serious follower" of that person or a "committed adherent." Others have correctly pointed out that, in the Greek text, there is only one primary verb in Jesus' command in Matthew 28:20 and that is the verb *disciple*. We should be very clear in our understanding that what Jesus really told us to do was to go into the world and, as we preach the Gospel, make converts of each people group (nation) into resolute followers of Him.

The Results of a Lack of Discipleship

Churches which change the world understand the importance of discipleship. They know new converts do not *automatically* become powerful Christians who will change the world around them. The leaders of world-impact churches realize converts must be carefully taught both *what* Jesus said and *how* to obey those instructions. They recognize also this process does not happen without serious effort.

Many churches, however, do not understand this truth, or at least they do not practice it. Generally we in the Body of Christ are not investing much time or effort in the vital task of discipleship, and for this we pay a great price. Often new converts do not develop into the strong, committed believers we would like them to be. Rather our churches are frequently filled with:

- Church members who are immature and who often fall away from Christ rather quickly.

- Church members who are not growing in their walk with God and who regularly do not develop godly character.

- Church members who neither tithe nor give significantly of their finances to their churches. (A person who *tithes* is one who gives at least 10% of his income to the church in order to help advance God's Kingdom on earth.)

- Church members who are not willing or able to take responsibility for the progress of the Gospel in their communities.

Most pastors and church leaders wish this were not so, but often put forth little effort to change it. Churches, however, which impact the world (*Great Commission Churches*) recognize the need for discipling new converts and actively work toward that goal.

Biblical Characteristics of a Disciple

To be truly effective in making disciples, leaders must first *see* in their mind and spirit what a true follower of Jesus should be. Before an artist can paint a picture, he must either be looking at something he wants to paint or he must see the picture clearly in his mind. Otherwise, he does not know what to paint on the canvas. Similarly, before we can successfully produce biblical disciples of Jesus in our churches, we must clearly recognize the qualities that make one a true disciple. I believe there are five vital *heart characteristics* of a devoted follower of Jesus. We must understand and ever remember that discipleship is a matter of reaching the *heart* of the new believer, not of teaching him to obey rules and regulations. These heart characteristics include the following:

- Disciples of Jesus have *surrendered* hearts. They have yielded their wills to Christ, acknowledging that He alone is Lord of their lives. They have forsaken all other gods and make decisions in life based on Jesus' will and direction.

- Disciples of Jesus have *growing* hearts. They are developing an intimate, growing, personal relationship with Jesus and are building godly character into their lives as they walk in daily obedience to Him.

- Disciples of Jesus have *servant* hearts. They are passionate about serving Christ and others. Their lives are no longer self-centered and they now live to serve God and people. This is their fundamental calling in life.

- Disciples of Jesus have *generous* hearts. They give liberally of all their resources—time, talent, money, and energy in the local church in order to help build God's Kingdom on earth.

- Disciples of Jesus have *evangelistic* hearts. They are vitally involved in reaching lost family and friends and in helping to complete *The Great Commission*.

How Paul Discipled Christians

A phenomenon of early church history is the way Paul the apostle was able to disciple new Christians so effectively that he could leave them, sometimes for years, to carry on God's work in their regions without his presence. He often did so in an amazingly brief period of time. Veteran missionary Roland Allen reminds us that Paul often preached in a place for a short period (five or six months) and then left behind a remarkably mature church capable of growth and expansion and one which did not need his direct involvement in order to do so. What was his strategy? Allen helps us uncover the answer as he relates the following characteristics of Paul's discipling method:

Part of Paul's strategy was his preaching and teaching. Allen points out that Paul never minimized the breach between following Jesus and heathenism. Repentance and faith, Allen says, were the keynotes of Paul's preaching. He declared that a disciple of Jesus was part of the Kingdom of God and the heathen part of the kingdom of evil. Paul understood the purpose of his preaching to be turning people from darkness to light and from the power of Satan to God. He knew that in repentance people confess that they have been walking in death and darkness; in faith they find the new way of life in Christ. In repentance people break with a sinful world, and in faith they enter God's kingdom.[1] Allen points out, from the first letter to the Thessalonians, that Paul's preaching and teaching characteristically contained the following elements:[2]

- There is one true and living God (1:9).

- Idolatry is sinful and must be forsaken (1:9).

- The wrath of God is ready to be revealed against the heathen for their impurity (4:6) and against the Jews for their rejection of Christ (2:15–16).

- God's judgment will come suddenly and unexpectedly (5:2–3).

- Jesus, God's Son (1:10) died for us (5:10), was raised from the dead (4:14), and is the Savior from God's wrath (1:10).

- The Kingdom of Jesus is now set up and everyone is invited to enter it (2:12).

- Those who believe and turn to God expect the Savior to return from heaven and receive them (1:10; 4:15–17).

- While they are awaiting Jesus' return, believers are to live lives which are pure (4:1–8), constructive (4:11–12), and watchful (5:4–8).

- In order to help them do those things, God has given believers His Holy Spirit (4:8; 5:19).

If we desire to be successful in making true disciples, as Paul was successful, leaders should change the focus of their preaching and teaching to follow Paul's example. Much preaching in the world today lacks scriptural depth and often deals with peripheral issues rather than laying a solid foundation for developing mature followers of Christ.

One secret of Paul's success lay in the very beginning of his work in a new area. The training of the first converts in the region where Paul was planting new churches established the pattern for future ministry. Roland Allen reminds us that Paul, in contrast to many missionaries today, taught people from the beginning to rely on God rather than on himself. Paul understood if the infant community of believers learned to depend passively on him for everything, the work would forever be handicapped. Instead of seeking strength and guidance from the Holy Spirit, they would seek it in Paul, thus putting him in the place of Christ.[3] If this happens, Allen says, the missionary will both retard the spiritual growth of converts and teach them to rely on the wrong source of strength. Paul's intent was to establish organized, indigenous churches which would not depend on him for oversight and finance. Allen proceeds to show that Paul's keys to discipling new believers lay in two areas—what he taught his converts and how he prepared them for baptism and ordination:

What Paul taught his converts (in the most simple and practical form):[4]

- The doctrine of God the Father, the Creator.
- The doctrine of Jesus, the resurrected Son of God, our Redeemer and Savior.
- The doctrine of the Holy Spirit, the indwelling source of our strength.
- An understanding of the life of Christ.
- An understanding of Holy Communion as it was revealed to him by the Lord.
- The meaning and necessity of Baptism, which Paul declared was not optional for believers.

Allen says that Paul, because of his itinerant ministry, was likely able to teach believers only these basic truths. It may be the simplicity and brevity of Paul's teaching which constituted its strength.[5]

How Paul prepared his converts for baptism and ordination:

Allen shows that very little knowledge of Christian truth was required by Paul as a condition for baptism.[6] For example, Paul baptized the jailor at Philippi and his family upon his simple confession of faith in Jesus after only an hour or two of instruction. Apparently, Paul allowed anyone who confessed his sins in repentance and acknowledged Jesus as Lord to be baptized. It should be understood, however, that it was not characteristic of Paul to allow converts to be baptized without any careful instruction at all or without understanding that they had indeed experienced genuine conversion. Paul's two requirements for baptism were repentance and faith.[7]

One of the most important elements of Paul's success was allowing the local church to decide who should and should not be baptized. We have made a tragic mistake, Allen states, in giving the missionary the entire responsibility for those decisions. The missionary, who is a stranger in the culture, is in the least capable position to ascertain the true motives and character of converts.[8]

Allen points out that Paul also gave the new church some responsibility in the appointment of elders (e.g., officially recognizing a candidate as a man of character and of good reputation).[9] Although our subject is discipling converts rather than the appointment and ordination of elders, this does help to reinforce that Paul intended to leave the group under the guidance of the Holy Spirit and under their own leadership instead of under his direction.

Suggestions for Effective Discipling

From my years of experience as a pastor and church leader and from my observation of effective churches throughout the world, it has become clear that the following things help produce mature and loyal followers of Jesus:

A well-designed but simple program of discipleship training should be an ongoing effort in the church. This can be done with each individual or with a group of new converts. Paul's teaching, as related above, may form the core of the instruction, along with the five *heart characteristics* of a disciple of Jesus discussed earlier in this chapter. Many churches conduct discipleship classes once or twice a week for several weeks. If your church does not have such a training program, the senior leadership should proceed to develop one quickly. An alternative plan for discipleship training is listed in the back of this book. (See Note 4 in the Appendix for a sample of a Discipleship Training Class recommended by David Garrison.)

Discipleship training should include teaching on the need for daily fellowship with Jesus. Early in the discipling process, believers need to see that the *purpose* of conversion is to bring them into deep relationship with the Father. God gave Christ to us in order to bring us to Himself. The young believer must be shown that he has no power of his own to live the Christian life and that the strength and inspiration to do so comes from daily, meaningful fellowship with the living God. As converts discover the value of taking time each day to be alone with God, they will experience His presence and learn the mystery of the power for living a godly life.

Discipleship training should include the subjects of *spiritual warfare* and *persecution.* When a person comes to Christ, especially if he is from a Muslim, Hindu, or Buddhist family, Satan often attacks by bringing persecution from family or relatives. Many new followers of Jesus are ostracized by family. Converts may not be aware of the spiritual forces at work when they are rejected by family members. Sometimes these young believers quickly become discouraged. Proper discipling of new believers will help them understand that every Christian is in a real battle with a real enemy—and also that Christ has given them power to be victorious in each conflict and to genuinely love and pray for those who persecute them (Matthew 5:43–48).

Small groups which meet regularly are important for new believers to build relationships with other believers for encouragement and accountability. Like new babies, new followers of Jesus are vulnerable and need the loving nurture of mature believers.

New believers should quickly be involved in one of the church's outreach ministries. This will help them develop a heart of love and concern for others. Jesus did not wait for His disciples to become mature before He involved them in outreach. He evidently "pushed them out" rather quickly. Outreach will help the young believer develop a focus on ministry to others rather than a self-absorbed, inward focus in life.

Young converts should get involved in the process of helping disciple other new believers as quickly as possible. New followers of Jesus do not have to be mature *before* they are involved in ministry. In fact, involvement in ministry is one of the things which help them *develop* maturity. Converts should learn to share with family and friends who come to Christ the things they are learning in their own spiritual journey with God.

It would be difficult to over-emphasize the value of discipleship training. Churches which impact the world take seriously the commands of Jesus and are diligently incorporating those commands into the life of their congregation. They learn to love and nurture immature converts and to quickly lead them to become powerful disciples of Jesus.

Words of Caution

Before leaving this subject, two words of caution are appropriate. The first is that we must not *complicate* the Gospel for converts. We must be careful not to teach the *tenets* of our faith rather than the faith itself. Jesus told us to teach His followers to obey the things which *He* taught. Many are aware of tragic mistakes some Western missionaries have made in the past—teaching the views of the Western world (or of their own denomination or group) rather than allowing the Gospel to progress naturally in the new culture to which they were sent. Western missionaries are not, however, the only ones who make this mistake. It is often made by national leaders in the Two-Thirds World as well, and we must exercise caution here.

The second word of prudence here is that we do not hinder the free flow of the Gospel by making the discipling process too long or too structured. The simplicity of Paul's plan is our example. In churches and ministries where new converts are set free to share their faith quickly, while the initial fire of conversion is still burning, growth is often explosive. New believers are released to fulfill their God-given destinies and are quickly maturing as they are involved in ministry outreach to family, friends, and neighbors. In other instances, the church is growing more slowly because there are too many restrictions placed on new believers. Releasing new converts into real freedom is difficult for those churches. Whatever system or method you choose for discipling new converts, they must be set free to become all *God* intends them to be and must not be restrained by institutional methods, ideas, and practices which have hindered the progress of some churches in the past.

Practical Application for Chapter Nine

1. Think about this chapter. Is your church effectively producing mature disciples of Jesus? Are most of your converts becoming the strong, powerful believers you desire? If not, why not? If so, what are the keys to your success? Take a moment to write them down.

2. Think through the list of five *heart-characteristics* of a disciple of Jesus. Is anything of importance left out? Are there additional characteristics that a true follower of Jesus should have? Be sure to base your answer on

God's Word. Also think about whether or not these are characteristic of your life personally.

3. Does your church already have an effective method for teaching new converts? If not, begin developing your discipleship program now. Be sure to base your teaching on Scripture and not on your own preferences. If you do have an effective discipling program, what are its essential elements?

4. Review the list of six suggestions for helping develop new converts. Which of these are you already doing? Are there other things that you need to be doing in order to help produce quality disciples of Jesus in your church?

5. In your plans for discipling new converts, please remember not to make the process too long, too complicated, or too structured. Teach the basics and release people in ministry.

ENDNOTES

1 *Missionary Method's—St. Paul's or Ours*, Roland Allen, p. 77

2 Ibid, p. 68

3 Ibid, p. 81.

4 Ibid, pp. 87-90.

5 Ibid, p. 90.

6 Ibid, p. 95

7   Ibid, p. 96-97

8   Ibid, p.98

9   Ibid, p. 99

DEDICATION TO CHURCH PLANTING

THE SIXTH CHARACTERISTIC OF GREAT COMMISSION CHURCHES

"...on this rock I will build My church, and the gates of Hades shall not prevail against it."

(Matthew 16:18)

The sixth characteristic of churches which change the world is that they are dedicated to planting new churches. Impact churches understand they cannot influence the world alone. They must have help and thus recognize the enormous value of planting new churches. *Great Commission Churches* realize the planting of new churches was the primary way in which Jesus, from the beginning, planned to extend His Kingdom to "Jerusalem, Judea, Samaria, and the ends of the earth."

The Expansion of God's Kingdom

Dr. C. Peter Wagner is correct when he says the planting of new churches is the most effective means under heaven for evangelizing lost people. Indeed, it is not only the most effective way; it is, to my knowledge, the only way that God's Kingdom can be effectively extended on a long term basis. A number of revivals of history were short-lived, in part because they did not result in the planting of new congregations through which the move of God could be preserved in the society.

Churches which are being planted around the world may look differently and operate with significant diversity in various countries and cultures. The fact remains, however, that the planting of new churches, whatever form they take, is vital for the evangelization of the world. Churches may be large or small, highly organized or relatively unorganized. They may meet in church buildings or in homes, but wherever they are, and however their members meet, they are both the primary manifestation of God's Kingdom on earth and His representatives in their communities.

Evangelists and Church Planting

It is crucial to understand the *goal* of the Church's mission is not simply evangelism, but rather the planting of new churches everywhere. It is also important that the tens of thousands of workers who refer to themselves as *evangelists,* especially in the Two-Thirds World, grasp this truth. What a difference it could make in our attempt to finish *The Great Commission* if evangelists in every country would understand that their evangelistic gifting and calling could be most effectively used in the context of church planting. If these evangelists will begin to perceive themselves as church planters and direct their energies toward planting dynamic churches in the unreached towns and villages of their countries, instead of simply preaching to believers in existing churches, we will finish the assignment Jesus gave us much more quickly.

Many workers throughout the world who call themselves evangelists are simply preaching to try and stir up the believers. While that may be a legitimate need, it is not the work of an evangelist. True evangelists win people to Christ. They preach to unbelievers, not to believers. And to be most effective, their ministries should focus on those who have not heard. Many evangelists should see themselves as workers who penetrate new areas with the Gospel of Jesus Christ by reaching and discipling people in unreached towns and villages in their areas and forming the new believers into house churches before moving on to another unreached community.

In his extensive ministry of training leaders in India, Dr. Paul (Bobby) Gupta, has discovered, however, that gifted evangelists are sometimes not gifted in the ability to disciple new believers or to oversee churches.[1] In this case, it will be important for evangelists to partner with other workers who have teaching and pastoral gifts in order to accomplish the goal of the church's mission— the planting of dynamic, new churches.

Paul's Church Planting in Ephesus

The commitment to church planting is one of the fundamental things which enabled the Apostle Paul to make an impact on the world. The *Seven Churches of Asia Minor* are listed in chapters one to three of *The Revelation,* the last book of the New Testament. They are Ephesus, Smyrna, Pergamos, Thyatira, Sardis, Philadelphia, and Laodicea. How were these churches started? They were, in all probability, the result of Paul's church planting efforts in the city of Ephesus. Paul's activity in Ephesus became one of the most effective church planting endeavors of his day. Not only did Paul plant a church which impacted the entire city, but he also planted the six other churches just mentioned during the three years he spent in Ephesus. These churches were *daughter churches* of the Ephesus church, likely formed as outreaches of the mother church. Through these churches Paul's ministry impacted the entire province of Asia Minor (what is roughly the nation of Turkey today). A wise leader, Paul understood the importance of church planting and was deeply committed to it throughout his ministry.

This commitment is also seen in the actions of the church at Antioch, especially in the sending out of their two most notable leaders into evangelistic/church planting ministry. Many churches might send some of their less significant leaders on such an assignment, but the Antioch church sent Saul and Barnabas (Acts 13:1–4). The Antioch elders and teachers were convinced of the importance of spreading the Gospel by starting new churches in areas where the Gospel had not yet been preached.

Churches Planting Churches

In order to finish *The Great Commission* in this generation, every church should follow Paul's example in Ephesus and the example of the Antioch church in evangelizing its community, province and country by planting other churches. Here is an important principle of life: *Everything which is living and healthy grows and reproduces itself.* That is true of goats and sheep and camels and trees and flowers—and people. My wife and I are living and healthy people and have reproduced ourselves by bringing three wonderful children into the world. Our children are also living and healthy and have now reproduced themselves and given us eight grandchildren. This reproductive characteristic should also be true of churches. Healthy churches should always be growing and reproducing by planting other churches in their own communities and by targeting unreached towns and villages which have no church. Many growing churches around the world are planting *multiple* new churches simultaneously, just as Paul did in Ephesus.

George Patterson reminds us that the goal of church planting must be the *spontaneous multiplication* of new churches. Patterson says it is crucial to plant the kind of churches which will grow and reproduce spontaneously—which will give birth to daughter churches, granddaughter churches, and great-granddaughter churches—without outsiders pushing them to do so.

Recently I spoke to a church in a large Asian city. Although the congregation is small (about 100 believers), it is no ordinary church. This *Great Commission Church* is alive with vision and passion to help reach their country for Christ. The church has eight branch congregations located both within and outside the city and is actively working to win and disciple people in each of these areas. Although eight branch churches is a large number for a congregation that size, the establishing of multiple new churches is characteristic of *Great Commission Churches* across the Majority World.

Six Stages of Church Planting

In order to understand church planting more fully, let me share briefly *Six Stages of Church Planting.*[2] You will see that planting new churches is somewhat like bringing a new baby into the world. Those six stages are as follows:

1. The Conception Stage. The first stage involves the initial idea of an individual or congregation deciding to plant a new church, together with the commitment to do so. In this stage, leadership develops the initial vision for the new church, recruits a team to help plant the church, and designs a basic strategy or plan for carrying out the project.

2. *The Development Stage.* The church planter will train his team for the project, start initial evangelism and discipleship outreach into the targeted village or area, and gather a core group of believers in the targeted community.

3. *The Birth Stage.* The church planter or church planting team will make preparation for the public meetings to commence. The new group of discipled converts will form the nucleus of the new congregation and a location for the public worship gathering will be secured. The place may be a home or a rented building, but careful plans for the weekly worship services should now be made and needed workers trained.

4. *The Growth Stage.* At this stage, the church planters will share the long-term vision for the new church which has now begun its public gatherings. The vision

should include small group ministry, effective evangelism, discipling new converts, and training leaders for the future growth and development of the congregation. The training of workers is one of our most important assignments and should be given serious attention at this stage.

5. *The Maturity Stage.* The church planter or pastor will now build a vision for *The Great Commission* into the heart of the congregation through his preaching, teaching, and the training of leadership in the new congregation. The church should now have effective small groups operating, good worship services, and effective evangelism outreaches into the community. The leaders who have been trained, and who are being trained, should now take responsibility in the areas of their gifting and calling as the church grows and develops. It should be remembered that one of the most significant challenges for most leaders is equipping, empowering, and releasing leaders under them to carry out the ministries God has given them. The training of leaders and the releasing of control of ministry to them is an idea that is foreign to most leaders. This obviously requires skill, insight, wisdom and courage, but it must be done if we are to expand the Kingdom and finish *The Great Commission* in this generation.

6. *The Reproduction Stage.* Please remember that everything which is living and healthy grows and reproduces. The congregation will now make plans to birth daughter congregations in neighboring towns and villages which are currently unreached with the Gospel. No church planting project is complete until the new church begins producing daughter churches in un-

reached areas. The Kekchi believers of Guatemala, in fact, say that a church which has no mission congregation is a dead church.[3] As more churches in a given area (or among a particular people group) commit themselves to the effort of birthing daughter congregations, potential is created for an enormous move of God to take place.

Just as new children who are born into a family need love, care, patience, and training, so do new churches. It is vital for newly-formed congregations to have proper oversight until they are able to function on their own. This supervision, however, as we saw with the Apostle Paul, is not required long-term if new workers are effectively discipled and trained.

Self-supporting, Self-governing, and Self-propagating

It is important to understand that established churches, as well as new church plants, must be self-supporting (not reliant upon outside organizations for finances), self-governing (not reliant upon outside organizations in decision-making), and self-propagating (not reliant upon outside organizations in order to evangelize their own people). Just as birthing a new church can be compared to bringing a child into the world, we must remember there comes a time in the life of every child when he becomes an adult and no longer depends on his parents. The adult child becomes responsible for himself in every way. The same is true with churches. Some Western missionaries in the past did a great disservice to the people to whom they were sent by planting churches which developed an artificial dependency on the West. This reliance was, in many ways, disastrous to the rapid spread of the Gospel in the new culture. Had these churches been taught to make their own way, trusting God to supply their needs, instead of developing an unhealthy reliance on the West (and upon the missionary himself), much more progress could have been made. We must not make this mistake again, but must develop works which are genuinely self-supporting, self-governing, and self-propagating.[4]

Missionary church planters, if they are to be most effective, must keep in focus that they should, as quickly as possible, train local leadership for the new work, release the work to them, and go on to another field.

Examples of Successful Church Planting

An explosion of church planting is necessary all over the world in order to reach the hundreds of thousands of towns and villages, especially in the Majority World, which have no churches. In India for example, at the time of this writing, there are more than 400,000 towns and villages which do not have a church of any kind. Thankfully, many groups and organizations have begun to comprehend the enormity of this need in India (and in many other countries) and are rallying their troops to meet it. Following are four examples of church planting ministries which are highly successful at present.

One ministry in Southeast Asia, at the time of this writing, is training 30 new church planters per year. To date they have trained 342 church planters and have established more than 300 churches in the past six years. Through the efforts of these church-planters, more than 15,000 Buddhists have been converted to Christ.

It is of interest that approximately 25% of the church planters in this organization are women. Their strategy includes the following:

- They conduct an annual *Institute of Church Planting* for 30 key leaders. These leaders are carefully selected because of their giftings, callings, and commitment to church planting from among the organization's current churches.

- These 30 church planters are trained at the mother church facility for two months. Lectures are given by church leaders along with guest lecturers skilled in church planting, in order to train the workers as effectively as possible. A different subject is taught each week during the two-month period.

- Following the two months of initial training, each trainee is sent to a designated unreached town or village to plant a new church. With this "on the job training," they immediately put into action the instruction they have received. One week each month they are brought back to the mother church facility for additional training. This phase lasts four months. When the church planters return for additional training, they are full of questions and this, of course, enhances the effectiveness of the instruction.

- Each trainee plants a new church in an unreached town or village as part of their training program.

- All of the organization's church planters meet once each month for a day of fasting and prayer at the mother church facility. The purpose of this meeting is prayer, fellowship, encouragement, and further training.

- The church planters continue to be mentored by the organization's current leadership.

One organization in southern Asia has trained 170 key leaders which they call *Timothy 1 Workers*. These leaders have trained 4,000 men and 3,500 women who are actively discipling others in the villages of a certain state and planting house churches. They have targeted each of the state's 107,000 villages and have set a goal to bring the Gospel to every home of every village in their state by 2010. Their strategy is called a "Block Strategy"[5] and operates as follows:

- First they research the area. Short-term research teams are sent to learn everything they can about the targeted town or village's people, customs, culture, and felt-needs (proper education for children, medicine to combat certain illnesses which are rampant in the village, jobs, ministry to widows and orphans, etc.). Ministering to felt-needs often opens a major door into the village or people group.

- Next they designate two *Strategy Coordinators* in each block of the state who identify 10 men and 10 women in their block for discipling.

- The workers are trained using a special discipleship curriculum designed to produce strong believers.

- They use both men (Timothy workers) and women (Esther workers) for the evangelism and discipleship process. Men disciple men and women disciple women.

- The goal is to establish house churches in every village of the block.

- The workers disciple self-supporting leaders to oversee the house churches.

- The primary emphasis of this organization is to produce strong believers and strong churches.

- They emphasize churches reproducing churches.

- They have an extensive and excellent program for reaching children through providing quality education.

Another organization in southern Asia has developed 90 training centers which are located in 14 states of their country. At any given time, more than 1,000 church planters are in training. This group is equipping an average of 10,000 workers per year. At the time of this writing, some 50,000 workers have been trained and their church planting efforts have resulted in 20,000 house churches in 14 states. The group has set a goal to plant a church in each of the more than 12,000 villages of their home state within the next four years. Their organizational strategy includes the following:

- The group operates a variety of training programs in order to accommodate more trainees. On average, 20–25 people come once each week to be equipped in each of their 90 centers.

- The focus of their training is "saturation church planting," and their goal is to plant a church in every district, tehsil, block, pin code, and village of targeted areas.

- Each trainee targets a village for church planting as a part of his training program.

- The philosophy of the organization, as it relates to *Unreached Peoples,* is to train people from various unreached groups, as they come to Christ, to reach their own people group through church planting, rather than training cross-cultural church planters.

One of many movements in China is referred to by Dr. David Garrison as the *Yanyin Movement.*[6] This work grew from three house churches with 85 members to 900 churches with nearly 100,000 worshiping believers in only 10 years. The movement was distinguished by extensive personal and mass evangelism, widespread lay leadership development, mutual accountability, and a model which can be rapidly reproduced. This was their strategy:

- The work was led by a missionary *Strategy Coordinator* from the USA who mobilized ethnic Chinese church planters from other countries to assist him in the endeavor. These church planters teamed with Yanyin believers from the small existing work to form new house churches in every county of the province.

- By 1998 the *Strategy Coordinator* left the work totally in the hands of the Chinese church planters and the Yanyin believers.

- The *Jesus Film* and widespread evangelism campaigns were used to identify inquirers for discipleship and teaching. The church planters concentrated on the heads of households.

- As people expressed interest in the Gospel, workers networked the extended families of these persons to expand their base, issuing invitations to study the Bible. After a few weeks of witness and evangelistic Bible studies, participants were invited to surrender their lives to Christ.

- Those who believed were quickly incorporated into discipleship studies for a few additional weeks, after which they were baptized.

- Church planters then identified people with leadership gifts and turned the leadership of the public meetings over to them. One of the church planters remained behind to mentor and further disciple these leaders for a period of time.

- These leaders then taught what they had learned to their house churches.

These are a few examples of groups which understand the value of, and which have a deep commitment to, church planting. Each of them has a good church planting strategy which is proving to be highly successful. The strategy you develop for your own church planting ministry may differ from these, or it may have some similarities to one or more of those discussed. The important thing is that you commit yourself to church planting in your own area. If you are part of a small organization or are an independent pastor or evangelist, please do not allow yourself be discouraged by the large statistics of some of these organizations. Numbers of churches are not the *only* measure of genuine success. The only way *The Great Commission* can be finished in this generation is for *everyone,* including you and me, to do his part. We must have the help of denominations and *Church Planting Movements* of all sizes, along with the tens of thousands of independent pastors, evangelists, and church planters located throughout the Two-Thirds World who will gain a vision for church planting.

Bringing God's Kingdom

As we are committed to planting the hundreds of thousands of new churches needed to finish *The Great Commission,* we must also focus on one of the primary *goals* of these new churches: to help bring God's Kingdom into the homes, villages, and cities of every ethnic group on earth. Jesus gave to His Church the "keys of the Kingdom" (Matthew 16:19). His purpose was to enable us to unlock every door of a society where people are held captive. When Jesus taught us to pray "Thy kingdom come," He was teaching us to pray (and work) for the release of every person who is in bondage to Satan. The "good news of the Kingdom" is that people can be set free from everything which keeps them from being all they were created to be. That freedom must be proclaimed in every home of every village and hamlet on earth. This is, of course, the *reason* we plant churches. We are not interested only in saving people from hell. We also want them to experience the life and liberation that Jesus came to bring. In this way we will help to bring God's Kingdom to every part of the earth and among every ethnic group in existence. May God help us to do so—and to do so quickly.

Practical Application for Chapter Ten

1. If you are currently serving as a pastor or the primary leader of a church, plan now to reproduce by planting new churches in your area and in unreached towns or villages near you. If you are an evangelist, think about what you can do to turn your evangelistic activities into church planting endeavors. Do you need to team up with someone who has a teaching or pastoral gifting in order to do this effectively?

2. Review the *Six Stages of Church Planting*. Think about how you would go about planting a new church in an unreached town or village. Ask God if this is something He would have you do. If so, which towns or villages will you target?

3. Think about the strategies of the church planting organizations which were referenced. Which of the four strategies appeals to you the most? Why? What can you do to incorporate those strategies in your own church planting endeavors?

4. Is your church planting multiple branch churches? If not, give this matter some serious and prayerful thought. If so, what is your strategy and how successful is it? Does it need to be modified based on new insight gained in this chapter?

5. How many churches do you think you can plant in your state or province among unreached towns and

villages during the next 10 years? How many can be planted through your entire organization? In calculating your answer, please remember that each church should reproduce itself regularly.

ENDNOTES

1   For a more complete understanding of what Gupta learned about gifted leaders in India, read his book entitled *Breaking Tradition to Accomplish Vision* (BMH Books, Winona Lake, IN, 2006)

2   *Planting Growing Churches for the 21st Century*, Aubrey Malpurs.

3   *Church Planting Movements*, David Garrison, p. 132.

4   *Church Planting Movements*, David Garrison, p. 82.

5   A "block" is a geographical division in this country which is normally comprised of 100-125 villages and 100,000-150,000 people.

6   A description of a *Church Planting Movement* in the Yanyin Province of China (not its real name) described by David Garrison in his book *Church Planting Movements* (WIGTake Resources, Midlothian, VA, USA).

COMMITMENT TO FINISH THE GREAT COMMISSION

THE SEVENTH CHARACTERISTIC OF GREAT COMMISSION CHURCHES

"Then He said to them, 'Thus it is written, and thus it was necessary for the Christ to suffer and to rise from the dead the third day, and that repentance and remission of sins should be preached in His name to all nations, beginning at Jerusalem.'"

(Luke 24:46–47)

The seventh characteristic of churches which impact their worlds is that they have a heart-commitment to help finish The Great Commission. These churches take seriously Christ's commands, including His final directive to disciple all the people groups on earth. Across the planet, independent local churches, denominations, ministry associations, and indigenous church planting organizations in the Majority World are becoming aware that *closure* (the finishing of *The Great Commission*) is possible. In order to finish the task in this generation, there must be an explosion of church planting activity in every country and which targets every unreached people group on earth.

A Population Explosion

A population explosion is going on in the world and has been for several generations. Presently, the population of the world is just over 6.58 billion and is growing at the rate of 240,000 per day. Most of that growth, however, has come in the past 100 years. In 1830 the world's population was approximately one billion. Interestingly, it took one hundred years (1830–1930) for the world to add one billion people. But then it took only 30 years to add another one billion people (1930–1960). The population explosion was beginning. From 1960–1975 the number of people went from three to four billion, thus taking only 15 years to add another billion. It then took only eleven years to add another billion population (1975–86) and 10 years to add another (1986–96). By 1996 world population was nearing six billion. The population explosion was now full-blown. Although this explosion has abated somewhat in the past few years, at the present rate of growth, it is projected that the world will have seven billion inhabitants by 2010.

Why is this understanding of population growth important? It is important in that it helps reinforce the fact that, if we are to finish *The Great Commission,* an explosion of church planting *must* become a reality. We must have tens of thousands of new churches in order to reach the people who are being born into the world each day, in addition to reaching the two billion already living who have yet to hear of Jesus' love and power to save. Much of this growth is, of course, in the nations of the Majority World where so many have not heard.

Global Population Statistics

At present, approximately 11% of the world's population are true believers. Another 22% are categorized as *nominal* followers of Jesus. Although they are counted in world population figures as being followers of Jesus, in reality they are only *supposed* followers. These people have never committed their lives to Jesus and are not following Him seriously. Another 39% of the world's inhabitants reside within reached people groups. Most of them have heard the Gospel but have made no commitment to Christ. The remaining 28% have not heard.[1] These are called *Unreached Peoples*. These two billion *Unreached Peoples* are comprised primarily of Muslim, Hindu, and Buddhist peoples, together with several non-religious or secular peoples of China and a few other communist countries.

Discipling the World's Unreached

It is vital that God's people come to understand that Jesus gave us a very clear mandate in *The Great Commission*. The mandate is to go into all the world and make disciples of every people group on earth. What kind of progress has been made in carrying out this assignment? How far do we have to go? At the time of this writing *Joshua Project* lists 15,899 different people groups in the world. Of these, 9,482 are categorized as *reached* people groups and 6,417 are considered *unreached* with the Gospel.

The definition of *Unreached Peoples* (UPGs) was given in chapter four. You may wish to review that chapter to refresh your memory. These groups must be specifically and intentionally targeted for church planting if we are to finish *The Great Commission.*

According to *Joshua Project,* the countries which have the largest numbers of *Unreached Peoples* are as follows:

1. India   4,000 (2,030)[2]

2. China   413

3. Pakistan   372

4. Bangladesh   331

5. Nepal   292

In our quest to disciple all the world's unreached people groups, we must give special attention to these countries for church planting, while not neglecting any of the other countries which have *Unreached Peoples.*

In order to finish *The Great Commission,* the three great religious worlds of Islam, Hinduism, and Buddhism must be reached for Christ. When categorized according to religion, 3,276 of the remaining UPGs are primarily Muslim. The Muslim groups include a total population of 1.3 billion. Hindus make up 2,426 of the groups and include approximately 900 million people. Another 555 of the UPGs are primarily Buddhist and encompass approximately 375 million people.[3] Hundreds of thousands of new churches must be planted among the peoples who make up these three great religious groups.

The vast majority of the unreached live in an area known in missions circles as the 10/40 *Window*. Within the 10/40 *Window* reside 60% of the world's population (3.7 billion people), the 55 least-reached countries, and 78% of those who have yet to hear the Gospel. Yet this area includes less than three percent (3%) of the world's missionary work force. Of the world's 420,000 current missionaries, only 10,000 are working among the least-reached peoples. If we are to finish *The Great Commission,* the 10/40 *Window* must be strategically targeted for church planting. Many missionaries from every part of the world must begin to concentrate on those people groups who have not heard. These *Unreached Peoples* must become our major focus for both prayer and church planting.

Much has been done during the past few decades to heighten the awareness of believers around the world to the needs of the unreached. Numerous projects have been undertaken by groups and organizations to help reach those who have yet to hear. In spite of the emphasis on the 10/40 *Window,* however, the needs of the unreached world have not found their way into the heart of the global missions endeavor. Even some of the renewed effort to reach them over the past few decades appears to be waning, at least in the West. According to the *World Evangelization Research Center* (WERC) and the *Global Evangelization Movement* (GEM), 95% of all discussion of missions currently focuses on the Christian world. An additional four percent (4%) of missions thought and emphasis focuses on the evangelized non-Christian world. However, less than one percent (1%) of all thinking, discussion, and action in the missions endeavor concerns ministry among the unevangelized or unreached. How tragic! How unbelievable! When will we awaken and come to our senses as a missionary movement?

Millions of Unreached are Dying

To further illustrate the numbers of people who have yet to hear the Gospel for the first time and who are dying without Christ, let me ask you to do something. Take the two forefingers of your right hand, place them on your left wrist and move them around until you find your pulse. Hold it there for a few moments and feel your heart beat. Do you realize that nearly every time your heart beats someone dies who has never heard about the love and grace of Jesus Christ? Meditate on that fact. Let it sink into your consciousness. Everyday more than 62,000 people die without once hearing an understandable presentation of the Gospel. The questions that need to be asked here are, "Do I really care?" and "Does this fact move me enough to do something about it?" The follow-up questions should be, "If I am indeed moved by this fact, what am I going to do?" and "How can I personally be involved in helping reach those who have yet to hear?"

Finishing the Great Commission

Churches that desire to make a real difference in the world are asking themselves these questions and are responding with definite action. A new emphasis on *finishing The Great Commission* appears to be arising, but it is happening largely in the non-Western Majority

World. It is here that the slumbering Church of Jesus Christ seems to be awakening with fresh vision and passion to finish the task. As stated in the "Author's Notes," although we cannot know with certainty exactly when *The Great Commission* will be completed, we can focus on creating a *Church Planting Movement* among each of the world's *Unreached Peoples.* That is what is happening more and more in the Majority World and, thankfully, these are primarily the people who will complete the assignment. There is a colossal need for the Western Church to awaken to the need and to fulfill its vital role in helping to finish *The Great Commission,* but the primary work will be done by the peoples of the Two-Thirds World.

Over the past 100 years, world-wide Christianity has made a decided and remarkable shift in its geographic center of gravity. At the beginning of the twentieth century, approximately 80% of all followers of Jesus lived in the West. At the close of the century, the percentage had decreased to approximately 45%. Contrary to popular opinion, the Body of Christ is experiencing a world-wide boom in the twenty-first century, but the majority of the growth is not in the West. Some who read this will be surprised to learn that in these early years of the twenty-first century a significant majority of Evangelicals are now located in the Two-Thirds World. They are neither white nor European nor Euro-American, and the percentage is increasing daily.[4]

For example, on the continent of Africa the number of Jesus' followers increased from 10 million to an amazing 360 million during the twentieth century. The number of Evangelicals continues to grow throughout the Two-Thirds World while continuing to decrease in the USA and Europe. It is apparent that both the center of gravity of the Church of Jesus Christ and the leadership of world missions are quickly shifting to the countries of the Majority World. Some would contend that the change has already taken place and that Christ's followers in these countries are already leading the way. It appears almost certain that the churches in the Two-Thirds World will play the leading role in finishing *The Great Commission*. Churches and missionaries in the West still have a significant part to play, but the primary work will be done by Jesus' followers who are located in the Muslim, Hindu, and Buddhist worlds.

Great Commission Churches all over the world understand these things and are committing themselves more and more to see the mandate from Jesus finished in this generation. They are beginning to rise to the challenge by directing more of their missions resources (time, energy, thinking, money, and personnel) toward the two billion persons who have yet to hear and they are specifically targeting the world's remaining *Unreached Peoples*. It is this kind of response that gives great encouragement and helps us believe the task can indeed be finished in this generation.

PRACTICAL APPLICATION FOR CHAPTER ELEVEN

1. Please stop and think about the fact that 28% of the world's population has yet to hear an understandable

presentation of the Gospel. How does that thought impact you? What if you and your family were among those who had not heard? Think about how different life would be for you.

2. How much attention are you and your church giving to church planting among the world's remaining 6,000+ *Unreached Peoples?* Do any of these UPGs live near you? Have you targeted any of them for prayer and church planting? If not, please begin now to make plans to do so. If so, which additional groups do you need to target?

3. If you are an independent pastor or evangelist, what you can do to reach out to the unreached towns and villages in your state or a neighboring state? If you are part of an organization or group of churches, discuss this issue with the leadership. Consider suggesting that your leaders read this book.

4. If you did not do the exercise of putting the two forefingers of your right hand on your left wrist and feeling your heart beat, please do so now. As you feel your pulse, pray for the 62,000 people who die daily without hearing of Jesus' love.

Endnotes

1 U.S. Center for World Mission (www.uscwm.org)

2 India has a total of 2,030 UPGs. When each of India's UPGs are counted and subdivided by state, the total is approximately 4,000. Many of these groups de-

velop different dialects and customs in the different states.

3 www.joshuaproject.net

4 See *The Next Christendom* (Phillip Jenkins, Oxford University Press) for a more complete study of this subject.

CLEAR STRATEGY FOR GROWTH AND EXPANSION

THE EIGHTH CHARACTERISTIC OF GREAT COMMISSION CHURCHES

"Then the Lord answered me and said: 'Write the vision and make it plain on tablets, that he may run who reads it.'"

(Habakkuk 2:2)

The eighth characteristic of churches which impact the world is that they have clear strategies for growth and expansion. These churches make a difference in the earth because they know what they are doing. They do not wander aimlessly through the world. Rather they run according to a plan which they believe has been given by God. These churches do not grow because their circumstances are conducive to growth or because other churches in their areas are growing. They would grow in almost any set of circumstances because they have both a passion to reach lost people and a wise plan for growth and increase. Their plans are clear enough that both the leadership and the majority of their members know them and can recount what they are. Clear vision and a *sense of destiny* drive these churches and unite their members.

In chapter ten, I gave four examples of church planting organizations from Cambodia, India, and China that have a deep commitment to church planting and clear strategies for implementing that commitment. These groups are not only *committed* to growth, they are very clear on *how* they will grow. Each has a defined track for their ministry. *Great Commission Churches* are like that.

The Strategy of Acts 1:8

It is my opinion that in Acts 1:8 Jesus gave His followers both a vision for the world and a simple, clear strategy for expanding His Kingdom throughout the earth. This plan was given specifically to the apostles whom Jesus trained. In a larger sense, however, it was also given to His followers of all time—to those who throughout the ages would believe Jesus' message and commit to the expansion of His Kingdom through the planting of new churches everywhere. This strategy is four-fold:

1. Jesus' followers were to be His witnesses (i.e. expand His Kingdom through evangelism, discipleship, and church planting) in *Jerusalem*. Jerusalem was the city where Jesus' disciples were located when the command was given and was to be their starting point and their base of operation. For present day followers of Jesus, *Jerusalem* is the place where we are living—our

city, town, or village. We also have been charged with the responsibility of reaching our home base (village/town/district/city) through evangelism, discipleship, and church planting, just as the apostles were charged with reaching theirs.

2. Jesus' followers were to be His witnesses (i.e. expand His Kingdom through evangelism, discipleship, and church planting) in *Judea*. Judea was the province of which Jerusalem was the capital. It was the next logical place for expansion. For us, *Judea* is the province or state in which our home base is located. Jesus' plan (and command) is for each of His followers to work beyond home. Our vision is to be broader than our immediate location. Each of us has been given the responsibility for targeting our entire province or state, as well as our local area, for church planting ministry.

3. The disciples of Jesus were to be His witnesses (i.e. expand His Kingdom through evangelism, discipleship, and church planting) in *Samaria*. Samaria was the neighboring province to Judea and was also to become a focus for the disciples' outreach ministry. Our *Samaria* is the states or provinces which border the one in which we are living. We also have a responsibility to target their unreached towns and villages for church planting ministry.

Samaria was, however, more than the neighboring province. It was also the place where the *unclean* lived—the foreign and despised people. The Samaritans were, in the minds of the Jews, *half-breeds*. The Jews detested these people and avoided contact with them at all costs. By including Samaria in His directive, Jesus was giving His disciples, both then and now, a radical command. He was telling them to *target* these lowly people (in the Jewish mind) for evangelism outreach. As we are aware, almost every society on earth has these despised groups which often become *hidden groups* within the culture. They are often overlooked for evangelism and church planting efforts. For example, the *Dalits* (*Harijans*)[1] of India are the *untouchables*—the lowest of the low of India's castes. They are so low, in fact, they are totally outside the caste system.

By including *Samaria* specifically in Acts 1:8, Jesus made sure that *no* people group would be left out of the disciples' outreach strategy, regardless of how lowly or despised they might be. So for us, Samaria not only represents the provinces or states which border our home state, it also includes the people groups which we tend to look down upon or consider unworthy of our attention. They too are loved by God and are to be targeted for evangelism and church planting.

4. Jesus' disciples were to be His witnesses (i.e. expand His Kingdom through evangelism, discipleship, and church planting) to *the end of the earth.* Jesus' Kingdom was to be stretched to every part of the world—to every tribe, nation, tongue and people. For us, *the end of the earth* is, first of all, the unreached people groups who live within the borders of our own country. We are entrusted by Jesus with the responsibility to disciple every *nation* (people group) living within our national borders. This part of Jesus' command clearly includes cross-cultural ministry. All of us (individuals, churches, and ministries) have the duty

to reach beyond our own cultural borders to the un-reached ethnic groups who live in our country. Once we have finished that assignment, *the end of the earth* will become the countries and people groups which border the country in which we live.

Great Commission Churches are committed to expanding God's Kingdom through strategic church planting ministry, both within their own cultural group and also among other cultures. As was stated earlier, they are involved in planting multiple new churches at any given time.[2] These churches understand that God's vision for the world includes every people group as a part of His Kingdom and are committed to help make that vision a reality.

Two Approaches to Reaching the Unreached

Already we have discussed church planting ministry. Now let's turn our attention to church planting ministry among *Unreached Peoples.* If we are to finish *The Great Commission,* planting churches where the Gospel has not reached must become a priority in the Body of Christ around the world. Each of the more than 6,000 ethnic groups which are officially categorized as *Unreached Peoples* must be strategically targeted for church planting endeavors. As I observe what is happening around the world, I see two primary approaches to cross cultural ministry and to reaching those who have not heard.

The first approach, which is being employed by some national church planting ministries in the Two-Thirds World, is one which does not primarily focus on *cross-cultural* missions. They believe that as they are carrying out their normal evangelism activities, people from different ethnic backgrounds are being gathered into the Kingdom, including some from unreached groups. These individuals come to the cities looking for work, to visit relatives, or for any number of reasons. They hear the Gospel and respond. Once they are converted, if they have a leadership gifting, they are then trained for evangelism and church planting and sent back to minister among their own people group. Some groups are seeing results from this approach which eliminates several of the difficult hurdles which have to be overcome for effective cross-cultural ministry to take place.

The other approach is to send cross-cultural missionaries from one people group to another. This practice has been done for centuries with varying degrees of effectiveness. It is my opinion that the remaining task (reaching two billion people in more than 6,000 *Unreached Peoples*) is so large that both approaches must be used. If *The Great Commission* is to be completed in this generation, there must be hundreds of cross-cultural missionaries from many different countries who will make the sacrifices required to reach the world's *Unreached Peoples*. One of the great needs, however, is not for *traditional* missionaries as we have always understood them, but rather for missionaries who serve *Strategy Coordinators,* a term adopted by Dr. David Garrison. The term is used to describe missionaries who take the responsibility to develop strategies for church planting which will enable an entire people group to come to faith in Jesus Christ (a *Church Planting Movement*).[3]

Strategy Coordinators are missionaries who do not

stay long-term with a people group. Rather, they develop the strategy for a *Church Planting Movement,* implement the strategy, train leaders in the people group, turn the work over to them, and move on to another unreached group. In so doing, they are following Paul's example of church planting which was described earlier. God is using this concept powerfully around the world to build His Kingdom and reach those who have not heard.

More and more we are coming to understand that the role of the cross-cultural missionary is not to plant churches among new people groups, but rather to facilitate *Church Planting Movements* by identifying, training, and releasing gifted people within the people group to lead the effort. Dr. Sherwood Lingenfelter reminds us:

> When the missionary becomes the church planter and not the facilitator of a church planting movement, he will attract individuals who are deviants from the local culture and are, most likely, more comfortable with the missionary's culture. Thus they lose the ability to establish a true church planting movement with the capacity to allow God to bring forth the necessary community transformation and to have intimacy with Christ.[4]

Lingenfelter goes on to say that the equipping of leaders in the targeted people group, empowering them to do the work, and releasing the control of preaching, teaching, evangelism, and prayer to them must happen at the very beginning of the work. Experience shows that most missionaries are not willing to do this—and thus suffer the consequences by stifling the new work.

Gene Daniels, in his fascinating book entitled *Searching for the Indigenous Church*[5] agrees and adds that most missionaries, including himself for many years, do not understand the meaning of the word *indigenous.* Through his own pilgrimage in this area, Daniels came to see that *indigenous* means a way of thinking that a foreigner will never completely understand and a culture which makes him so uncomfortable that he normally is not willing or able to allow the new work to be truly indigenous. In the book Daniels gives keen insight both into what an indigenous church looks like and into the major obstacles missionaries must overcome to form one.

Adopting Unreached Peoples

How do we target *Unreached Peoples* for church planting with some degree of effectiveness? Let me hasten to say that it is not my objective to discuss cross-cultural ministry in depth in this book. To do that effectively would require another entire volume.[6] The goal here is to give a few pointers on how the Body of Christ might do cross-cultural ministry in order to help reach the world's remaining unreached ethnic groups. One need is for thousands of churches and organizations all over the world, and especially those in the 10/40 *Window,* to *adopt* specific *Unreached Peoples* for prayer and for church planting outreach. Only as we target these unreached groups one at a time can we expect to make significant progress in our quest to finish *The Great Commission* in this generation.

Significant progress has been made in the past two or three decades, especially as it relates to targeting these groups for prayer. Much more, however, remains to be done in targeting them for effective church planting. If each church or organization would adopt one or two unreached people groups, target them for prayer and for church planting, and help generate a *Church Planting Movement* among them, we could finish *The Great Commission* more quickly than we often realize. One example is India, which has more *Unreached Peoples* than any other country. The task of evangelizing India's 4,000 unreached people groups seems overwhelming.[7] Yet India as a whole has nearly 100 evangelical churches for *each* unreached group within the bounds of the country. Mathematically speaking, the job could be finished rather quickly if the concept of adopting unreached people groups would be embraced by the majority of India's churches. The same is true, of course, for almost every other country where there are significant numbers of unreached ethnic groups.

The Difficulty of Near-Neighbor Evangelism

One word of caution needs to be mentioned at this point. Dr. Ralph Winter raises an interesting issue which complicates cross-cultural ministry when he reminds us of what he refers to as a "little-understood fact about missions." That fact is the difficulty of *near-neighbor evangelism.* According to Dr. Winter, most of the world's people groups tend to be alienated from the other ethnic groups which live around them. These groups often have little interaction with one another and regularly have animosity toward each other. This makes it challenging to do missionary work among near-neighbors. Winter illustrates this point by saying that it would be easier for a Navajo missionary in the USA to be effective among Laplanders in Norway than among his neighboring Hopi Indian tribe. According to Dr. Winter, this is one of the most unavoidable obstacles in missions work today.

This "near neighbor" challenge should be taken into consideration as we contemplate how to finish *The Great Commission.* It may, in fact, have significant bearing on *where* we send our missionaries. Perhaps churches in every country should consider sending missionaries to groups which are *not* near-neighbors and not send them to those ethnic groups which have hostility toward them. As we contemplate sending church planting missionaries among unreached people groups, we must keep in mind the difficulty of near-neighbor evangelism and not rely too heavily on national missionaries reaching the unreached groups who live around them. We must, however, continue to encourage God's people in every country to send missionaries to other countries and to diverse people groups as they have done for centuries.

Practical Steps for Targeting Unreached Peoples

The task of finishing *The Great Commission* is so large that it is going to require the help of all God's people. Every believer must become genuinely concerned and committed to the task of reaching the remaining *Unreached Peoples.* If we are to effectively target (or *adopt*) these groups for church planting outreach, it will require several simple but significant steps:[8]

First is the need to *prepare* for successful cross-cultural ministry. Preparation begins with an awareness of the need for cross-cultural ministry. Information about the more than 6,000 unreached ethnic groups, the two billion unreached people, and the 62,000 people who die daily without hearing the Gospel has been sufficiently discussed. It is imperative that this understanding deeply penetrate the hearts of God's people everywhere, resulting in firm commitment to cross-cultural church planting. The need must be seen clearly and felt deeply if we are to have sufficient passion, commitment, and endurance to carry out the assignment Jesus gave us.

Preparation also involves prayer that is fervent and consistent. Ask God which unreached group or groups He wants you to target. If this kind of mission is to be successful, the sending group must have the conviction that *God* is giving them the assignment. If you or your group is contemplating the adoption of an unreached people group for cross-cultural church planting ministry, the place to begin is in prayer. Ask God to show you which group or groups you are to adopt and to give you confirmation so you can proceed with courage and conviction, keeping in mind the difficulty of *near-neighbor evangelism*.

The second step is to *organize* properly for the mission, which involves the following things:

Do thorough research. Everything possible must be done to gain vital information about the people group (or unreached town or village) which you are targeting for church planting. Some of the things to look for include the obvious, such as the religion and the language of the group. Other things to look for include cultural distinctives of the people, humanitarian needs among them (food, clean water, common illnesses, etc.), educational needs, and other felt-needs of the group. Meeting these social needs will often open doors into these groups for evangelism and church planting.

This research can be done in several ways. The internet is an excellent source of information. Data on *Unreached Peoples* is available here from research which has been going on for the past several decades. At the close of this chapter several internet sites will be listed where research might begin. Short-term teams (to be discussed in the following chapter) can also be sent to the targeted group or village for the purpose of gathering specific information.

Team up with other ministries if possible. Occasionally the sending group can join with other organizations such as *Youth With A Mission, Operation Mobilization, Campus Crusade for Christ,* or *Jesus Film Teams* which have targeted the same unreached group or village. Often these evangelistic organizations are not directly involved in church planting themselves and would welcome a partnership with a group who would remain in the village or among the group for extended ministry.

Formulate a strategy. The plan may be simple or complex depending on the size and resources of the cross-cultural ministry team. It might initially involve a benevolent program to help meet humanitarian needs of the people group. It is important to have a good plan which is born out of prayer, involves proper research, and offers good potential for success. The strategy must include the elements of evangelism, discipling new converts, leadership development, and the formation of churches. It should also be a plan which is easily re-produced and which offers good opportunity for rapid multiplication among the group. It is helpful for the cross-cultural missionary, from the beginning, to see himself more as a *Strategy Coordinator* rather than as a traditional missionary. His job is to find, equip, and release leaders in the people group as rapidly as possible. He must not see himself as the church-planter, but rather as the facilitator of church planting which will be done by the people themselves.

Intercede for the group or village being targeted. Remember that the great battles of life are fought and won in prayer. The entire church or organization of the sending group should be mobilized to intercede for the targeted people or village. God does amazing things in answer to prayer.

The final step is to *implement* the strategy which has been formulated. The implementation stage includes the following:

Set timelines for executing the strategy. Timelines simply tell *when* the key elements of the strategy will be performed. It is important to set those timelines so that significant parts of the strategy do not get overlooked or unnecessarily delayed.

Continue to do research. One must never stop learning about the targeted group or village. Newly-discovered information about the ethnic group can sometimes be the difference between success and failure.

Continue the intercession. Once a *Strategy Coordinator* has been sent to the targeted group or village, the prayer must continue. The missionary coordinator should, in fact, regularly communicate prayer needs to the sending group so that intercessors can pray with understanding.

Identify and train Strategy Coordinators. More will be written about this in the next chapter. Please understand that these are two of the most important items in the entire process. Without the proper *selection* of gifted missionaries and without their proper *training,* the mission is doomed to failure.

Carry out the strategy step-by-step. Once a good strategy is in place and timelines are set, the only thing left is to implement the strategy in prayer and faith.

Update the strategy periodically. Strategies are designed to change as new information becomes available and new insights are gained. Do not hesitate to update or to alter your plan. Once each six months the strategy should be re-examined and changes made where appropriate.

Church Planting Movements

The goal of missions is to launch indigenous people movements among each of the world's ethnic groups which are capable of rapidly multiplying congregations so that the entire group is incorporated into the Body of Christ. That is indeed happening through one of the revolutionary things that God is doing in these last days among a number of the world's least-reached peoples. Every missionary, wherever he is laboring, should seek to grasp this work of God which is helping to reach these precious peoples more quickly than anyone ever thought possible. This work is often referred to as a "Church Planting Movement." In his outstanding book by that title,[9] Dr. David Garrison introduces the subject by giving the following staggering but well-documented statistics:

- In a certain country of East Asia, one ministry reported the planting of some 360 churches in six months with more than 10,000 baptisms taking place.

- In Latin America, a group overcame momentous governmental persecution and grew from 235 churches to more than 4,000 with more than 30,000 converts ready for baptism.

- Among the Bhojpuri speaking peoples of India, more than 4,000 new churches were planted and 300,000 believers were added to the kingdom in the decade of the 1990s.

- A missionary in Africa, after spending 30 years in planting four churches, reported 65 new church plants in nine months.

- In a certain Muslim country of Asia, more than 3,000

Isa Jamaats (Jesus Groups) were formed through which 150,000 Muslims became followers of Jesus.

- In Southeast Asia an organization grew from 85 members to 90,000 baptized members in just seven years, planting 920 new churches in the process.

- A missionary in North India saw a church planting movement explode from 28 churches to more than 4,500 churches with an estimated 300,000 confirmed believers in just eleven years.

What are *Church Planting Movements* and how do they spread so swiftly among a people group? In chapter five, a *Church Planting Movement* was defined as "a rapid multiplication of indigenous churches planting churches that sweeps through a people group or population segment."[10] David Garrison boldly declares: "Without exaggeration we can say that Church Planting Movements are the most effective means in the world today for drawing lost millions into saving, disciple-building relationships with Jesus Christ."[11] Garrison lists several characteristics which tend to define *Church Planting Movements* and explain how they operate. These include the following:

The rapid reproduction of churches among the people group. Strategies are developed which allow churches to birth daughter churches quickly. This vision and commitment is built into the very life of the movement. *Every* church rapidly duplicates itself by producing other churches in neighboring communities.

The formation of house churches rather than dedicated church buildings. This eliminates the necessity of raising large amounts of money for building construction and allows the groups to spread rapidly since they tend to operate on an extremely low budget. It also allows them to function without calling undue attention to themselves. When churches are planted in areas where there is intense persecution, this is vital.

Multiple, unpaid, indigenous lay leadership instead of professional clergy. Local leaders are quickly developed and entrusted with the future of the movement. This allows the work to rapidly expand without having to raise large amounts of money to pay pastors and without having to send them for extended training periods. It also helps to eliminate the gap between clergy and laity.

Extraordinary prayer. Earnest prayer permeates every aspect of *Church Planting Movements.* It is the first priority of both the strategists behind the movement and the people themselves. These people earnestly ask God to work His miracles in every aspect of life and ministry.

Having the Bible translated into the heart-language of the people group. This allows the Gospel to be understood more clearly by the new believers and helps avoid the movement being seen as a *foreign* religion among the group.

The authority of God's Word. This keeps the movements

from fragmenting and helps to keep them pure. Since this inner conductor is independent of the missionary, it does not require the missionary's presence for the movement to advance. The joint tracks of Scripture and the Lordship of Jesus help guide the movement into the fullness of God's plans and purposes.

Encouraging the indigenous believers to form their own expressions of worship. When the groups write their own hymns and praise songs and create other expressions of worship familiar to their culture, it helps the people feel comfortable with the Gospel and understand that it is not a Western religion imported into their culture. This is vital for rapid expansion of the movement in the society. Without this indigenous characteristic, the people group will often consider those who follow Jesus traitors to their family and culture.

Churches which are self-governing, self-supporting and self-propagating. Creating external dependency of any kind seriously hinders the rapid expansion of the Gospel among a people group and must be avoided at all costs. This is one of the serious mistakes made by some Western missionaries in the past. Often missionaries have been one of the forces which have impeded the formation of indigenous churches, sometimes because of their reluctance to turn loose of control, and sometimes because they are bothered by the structure and worship forms of the contextualized church.[12] At times, in fact, the missionary is embarrassed that the churches do not resemble their organizational or denominational pattern for churches.

The rapid assimilation of new believers into the life and work of the church. As this is done, more manpower is readily available. This must happen if the work is to be able to grow quickly. If the movement is to produce the hundreds of new churches needed to deeply impact the people group, then many new workers must be trained and released as swiftly as possible.

Missionaries taking the role of Strategy Coordinators[13] rather than a traditional missionary role. These *Strategy Coordinators* are, according to Dr. Garrison, missionaries who take the responsibility to develop the strategy for church planting which will enable the entire people group to come to faith in Jesus Christ. These cross-cultural workers often bring the vision, passion, and training required for the *Church Planting Movement* to be launched and then quickly pass it on to the people themselves. Then the Strategy Coordinator leaves.

Garrison shows that at the heart of a *Church Planting Movement* is the formation of House Churches—small fellowships of believers which spring up quickly, rapidly reproduce, and are led by unpaid lay leadership. This often enables the work to grow without expensive building and maintenance of church structures and without having to support a professional clergy. Garrison lists ten benefits of House Churches forming the core of such a movement:[14]

- Leadership responsibilities remain small and manageable.

- If heresies occur, they are confined by the small size of the house church.

- It is difficult for people to *hide* in a small group, so accountability is amplified.

- Member care is easier because everyone knows everyone else in the group.

- Because house church structure is simple, it is easier to reproduce.

- Small groups tend to be more efficient at evangelism and assimilation of new believers.

- Meeting in homes positions the church more closely to the lost.

- House churches tend to blend into the community, making them less vulnerable to persecution.

- Operating out of homes keeps the church's attention on daily life issues.

- The very nature of rapidly multiplying house churches promotes the swift development of new church leaders.

Church Planting Movements are normally led, as we have said, by missionaries who operate as *Strategy Coordinators* rather than in the traditional missionary role. These missionaries, according to Garrison, often consciously operate in a four-stage process of *Modeling, Assisting, Watching, and Leaving.*[15] Following the pattern of Paul which was described earlier, they *model* the evangelism, discipleship and church planting patterns which they desire the new believers to imitate; appoint, train, and *assist* the new leaders which are quickly chosen from the new believers to follow the model; *watch* to see that the new believers have caught the vision and plan and are reproducing successfully; and then *leave* the work in the hands of the leaders as quickly as possible and move on to new territories. Admittedly, leaving can be difficult for some missionaries. However, Garrison says, this is absolutely essential for the proper development of the movement. The Apostle Paul would likely agree. Some missionaries forget that one of their primary responsibilities is to work themselves out of a job. As the *Strategy Coordinators* do this, they teach the people to look to the Lord rather than to the missionary for future direction.

Donald McGavran similarly gives seven wise principles which missionaries should adopt in order to insure that churches planted in new cultures truly become indigenous and that they become "people movements" rather than a few isolated, ostracized churches. Those principles are as follows:[16]

- Aim for a cluster of growing congregations. Never be satisfied with a small group of churches. Make it your goal to reach the entire people group with indigenous congregations.

- Concentrate on one people group at a time. Endeavor to reach the entire society before moving on to another group.

- Encourage converts to remain with their people. Don't let the movement become "foreign" in the thinking of the people.

- Encourage group decisions for Christ. Ostracism is

much more difficult against a large group than against single individuals.

- Aim for a constant stream of new converts. Don't be satisfied with a few isolated believers. An ever-flowing stream of converts will come into healthy *Church Planting Movements.*

- Help converts exemplify the highest hopes of their people. Find out the true moral values of the people group and show the following of Jesus to be the best way for those values to be realized.

- Emphasize brotherhood. Help the people to see that every member of the group is important to God and that no one is favored over another.

Through *Church Planting Movements* entire people groups are coming to Christ and are developing an unusual degree of integrity, vibrancy, maturity, and commitment in a very short period of time. Every missionary who desires to work among unreached people groups should study this model carefully.

Bridges of God

Another important element of strategy has been called "bridges of God" by church-growth pioneer, Donald McGavran. Dr. McGavran and others realized, from studying the writings of the Apostle Paul, that Paul often moved about in the world according to relationships which developed with certain individuals. These relationships became *bridges* which opened new territories to the Gospel. Often there are more relational bridges in a congregation or group than are realized. In most congregations, especially in the Two-Thirds World, there are many people who speak multiple languages, who intermarry with individuals from various people groups, or who have family or friendship connections with other ethnic groups, some of which are unreached. These relationships can create links with new ethnic groups and unreached villages for the spread of the Gospel. Often it is God Himself who is creating these bridges so that His Kingdom may be expanded and we need to pay attention to what He is doing.

One good illustration from Scripture of a "bridge of God" is Jesus' encounter with the woman of Samaria (John 4:1–42). His conversation with the woman led him to remain in the city for two extra days in order to reap a harvest of Samaritans coming to faith. Another example is Philip's encounter with the Ethiopian man which resulted in the penetration of the Gospel into the continent of Africa (Acts 8:26–40). We must always be alert to these doors of opportunity which God sovereignly opens in order to bring the Gospel to those who have not heard.

Pioneer missiologist Roland Allen said, "The church that does not have a vision to conquer the world soon dies." How true. Churches which impact the world do indeed have a vision to make a difference in the world. They also have strategic plans by which this vision is accomplished. By contrast, the world is full of *ordinary* churches which have little vision and no plan for growth and expansion. These churches do indeed often die.

Internet websites are available where research on *Unreached Peoples* can be done. If you are unfamiliar with the internet, perhaps a young person in your church could be given the assignment of gathering information once your targeted group is selected. Some of those websites are as follows:

www.joshuaproject.net

www.partnersinternational.org

www.win1040.com

www.asiaharvest.org

www.ethnicharvest.org

www.gmi.org

www.gmi.org/ow

www.uscwm.org

www.imb.org

www.globalchristianity.org

www.jesusfilm.org

www.worldchristiandatabase.org

www.churchplantingmovements.com

Practical Application for Chapter Twelve

1. Review the strategies of the four church planting organizations given in chapter ten. Do you have a strategy for growth and expansion for your church or organization? If so, what is it? If not, please pray about working on one now. Examining these four strategies should get you going in the right direction.

2. Think about the vision and strategy given by Jesus in Acts 1:8. Do you presently have a vision for your *Judea, Samaria,* and the *ends of the earth?* Do you have a plan for church planting outreach in those areas? If so, what is your plan? If not, please seek the Lord diligently and develop a strategy to reach them.

3. Have you specifically targeted an unreached people group for church planting? If so, which group have you chosen? If not, please begin praying now, and ask God to lay one of the groups in your state or country (or another country) on your heart. Then begin making plans to reach them. Follow the suggestions given in this chapter. Be sure to include the people groups who would be *Samaritans* for you and consider what was said concerning the difficulty of near-neighbor evangelism.

4. If you are already committed to cross-cultural church planting ministry and have targeted a UPG, please read *Church Planting Movements* by David Garrison (WIGTake Resources, Midlothian, VA, USA). You may wish to check the website www.churchplanting-movements.com for more information.

5. Do you have relational "bridges" to any *Unreached Peoples* in your church? If so, what do you need to do about it? Is God opening doors for ministry to the unreached?

ENDNOTES

1   Formerly the *Dalits* (or Harijans) were referred to as *Bhangis* or *Chamars* or *Churas* – terms which are no longer acceptable in Indian society. *Dalits* ("people of the land") is a name these people have taken for themselves. *Harijans* ("children of God") is a name given them by Mahatma Gandhi.

2   Keep in mind when we say that each church should be planting multiple new churches, we are not talking about full-grown churches which have a full-time pastors and church buildings. Although some of them may eventually grow to the place where they have a building and a paid pastor, many will continue to function as House Churches which are led by unpaid, non-professional pastors or leaders.

3   A "Church Planting Movement" was defined in chapter three. It is a term coined by Dr. David Garrison to describe a rapid multiplication of indigenous churches planting other churches that tends to sweep through entire people groups.

4   *Breaking Tradition to Accomplish Vision* (Gupta and Lingenfelter), 2006, p. 60.

5   William Carey Library, Pasadena, CA, USA, 2005.

6   Gupta's and Lingenfelters' book entitled *Breaking Tradition to Accomplish Vision* (BMH Books, Winona, IN, USA, 2006) is very helpful at this point and gives a case study of how Gupta's church planting organization in India became effective at cross-cultural church planting.

7 The total number of unreached people groups in India, according to *Joshua Project*, is approximately 4,000 (when each group is counted separately in each of India's states).

8 I am grateful to Dr. Howard Foltz and his *Harvest Connection* teaching for insight into this area of training.

9 *Church Planting Movements*, David Garrison: WIGTake Resources, Midlothian, VA: 2004.

10 *Church Planting Movements*, David Garrison, p. 21

11 Ibid, p. 28

12 Often the primary problem here is that if a work starts to truly become indigenous, the missionary begins to feel so uncomfortable with the church he has produced that he will not release it to become what God intends. An added problem comes when representatives (or supporters) arrive from the missionary's culture and they too feel uncomfortable. This puts added pressure on the missionary.

13 *Church Planting Movements*, David Garrison, p. 17.

14 Ibid, p. 192-193.

15 Ibid, p. 194

16 *Perspectives*, 1999 Edition, pp. 399-401

Sending Trained Laborers into the Harvest

The Ninth Characteristic of Great Commission Churches

"And the things that you have heard from me among many witnesses, commit these to faithful men who will be able to teach others also."

(2 Timothy 2:2)

The ninth characteristic of churches which impact their worlds is that they send trained laborers into the harvest fields. These churches have learned a great secret. They know the value of providing quality training for their workers. The reason their churches and organizations continue to grow, expand, and operate with effectiveness is not a mystery. In one sense, they "make it happen," or they "set themselves up" for success by spending a great deal of time, effort, and money in training leaders and workers. They understand, as Dr. John Maxwell reminds us, that "in God's kingdom, everything rises and falls on leadership."

If you are a leader in God's Kingdom, please listen when I say that the size and quality of the work you are able to build depends primarily on your ability to effectively train leaders. In order to accomplish great things for God, a large vision for ministry is needed and passion is essential in order to carry out the vision, but these two qualities alone are not enough. As I travel throughout the Majority World, I often find leaders who have plenty of vision and a commitment that is unquestioned. But their churches and organizations are not growing as quickly and as solidly as they might, and they are not planting new churches as successfully as they could. Frequently, the reason is that they have not trained and released workers effectively enough to make their dreams and goals a reality. Most church leaders really *want* their churches to grow faster and larger, and they often desire to plant more and healthier churches, but their efforts produce mediocre success. They desire to reach out to *Unreached Peoples* in their areas, but are not able to do so effectively. One of the most common reasons is that they are not training quality leaders in the mother church and are not sending well-trained workers into the harvest.

Setting Goals

Let's talk about setting two goals, just to insure that we have clear vision and understandable objectives in this area. Proverbs 29:18 says, "Where there is no vision, the people perish." Around the world I find churches everywhere which are dying because of a lack of clear vision and purpose. If you are a pastor or the primary leader of a church or group of believers, consider setting the two following goals:

Goal #1: To send at least ten percent (10:100) of your adult church members into evangelism and church planting ministry. People who have studied spiritual gifts find that, in most churches, approximately 10% of believers have an evangelistic gift. Therefore this goal seems reasonable, especially for those working in the Two-Thirds World. If you have 50 adult members, your goal should be to train and send at least five workers into church planting outreach. If you have 500 members, your goal should be to send out 50 evangelists and church planters into the unreached towns and villages in your area.

Goal #2: To send at least one percent (1:100) of your people into full-time *cross-cultural* church planting ministry as *missionaries*.[1] If you have 100 adult members or less in your congregation, your goal should be to adopt one unreached people group and effectively train and send at least one missionary (*Strategy Coordinator*) to them. If you have 1,000 members, your goal should be to send at least 10 Strategy Coordinators into church planting among your country's unreached ethnic groups.

Effectively Training Leaders

For most churches these will be acceptable goals and this is a place to begin. With those goals in mind, let's talk about *how* to train leaders (evangelists/church-planters/Strategy Coordinators) effectively. In this book we can reference only a few of the high points of leadership training. Volumes of books have been written on effective leadership development and more are needed. However, my brief remarks in this chapter are directed to the training of cross-cultural missionaries who will work as *Strategy Coordinators* among *Unreached Peoples*. Most of the principles, however, will also apply to training church planters who will work among their own people groups.

The proper training of missionaries involves five simple stages which will help to improve our effectiveness.[2] If we are to finish *The Great Commission,* thousands of new missionaries must be trained and sent from our churches to the people groups who have yet to hear. The five basic stages of training are as follows:

1. The Interest Stage:

As you preach and teach on becoming a *Great Commission Church,* you will find that interest in becoming a church planter or a missionary/*Strategy Coordinator* will increase significantly. People respond to challenges they are given by the church's leadership. As men and women respond to the challenge, it is the responsibility of church leaders to confirm which potential workers are genuinely gifted and called by God to cross-cultural ministry. Some will respond initially to challenges from church leaders for which they are neither gifted nor called. The church leadership should meet with each potential missionary who indicates an interest in this kind of ministry in order to verify the gift and call of the individual. God will give your leaders wisdom and discernment to make those decisions. Those who respond, but are not genuinely gifted or called to be missionaries or church planters, should be directed into a ministry for which they are suited. Those whom the leaders recognize to be called to missionary work should immediately be given an initial assignment which involves both prayer and study about missionaries and church planters.

If your church does not have missions books, buy some. Use some of your church monies to purchase a few good biographies of missionaries or other good training books. You may also ask other pastors if you may borrow some. Perhaps they have books that they would be willing to lend. You may also check with missionary organizations which operate in your area (*Youth With A Mission, Operation Mobilization, Campus Crusade for Christ, Jesus Film Teams*) for books which could be borrowed until your church is able to establish its own missions library. Giving these candidates biographies of great missionaries is a good place to begin.

2. THE DISCIPLESHIP STAGE:

Once missionary candidates have been approved by the church leadership and initial prayer and reading assignments have been finished, the candidate should move into the next phase of training. There should be additional meetings with church leaders for counseling and guidance. In these meetings, leaders can help trainees clarify their calling from God, discern where the trainee is in his spiritual and character development, and give assignments in areas where he needs to grow.

The trainee should be given opportunity, if possible, to get initial cross-cultural ministry experience. He may be included as part of a short-term team from the local church to an unreached people group or be part of a *YWAM, OM,* or *Jesus Film* team which is working in an unreached area. This exposure to cross-cultural ministry will help confirm the missionary call of the trainee and give him valuable training. (Please remember that God calls and uses both men and women as missionaries in His kingdom.) The candidate should then be given additional and more intensive prayer, reading, and study assignments, especially in the area of cross-cultural ministry. One highly recommended book for missionary preparation is *Church Planting Movements* (David Garrison) which was discussed in the last chapter.

3. THE TRAINING STAGE: (THREE MONTHS TO FIVE YEARS)

As the trainee completes the *Discipleship Stage,* he should begin a period of formal training for missionary work. This stage may include an intensive course at a church planting school or a Bible college/university and/or seminary degree, depending on the requirements of the sending church or organization.[3] It is important to note that Dr. Sherwood Lingenfelter, after much research and observation, has concluded that "formal education is ill suited and cannot effectively equip evangelists, church planters, and apostolic leaders for ministry."[4] I tend to agree.

An illustration of this ineffectiveness is given

by Dr. Paul (Bobby) Gupta of the training ministry begun by his father (Hindustan Bible Institute, in
Chennai, India). After careful examination, Dr. Gupta
concludes:

> The more we evaluated the programs and policies of
> accreditation, the more we realized that we had sold
> our birthright. HBI was now serving the purposes
> of the university. Our leaders had compromised his-
> toric commitments to the Word of God, to building
> leaders of character and passion for reaching the lost,
> and to expanding Christ's church. We had sacrificed
> our vision to disciple the nation on the altar of estab-
> lishment interests for the legitimacy of programs and
> degrees.[5]

Such has been the case all too often in the Body of Christ.
Bible Colleges and training institutions almost without
number, and in most every part of the world, have di-
gressed significantly from the original vision given them
by the Holy Spirit in order to pursue the god of formal
education (and legitimacy in the minds of some). In so
doing many have lost the vision, the passion, and the
anointing that characterized their ministries in the beginning. The tragic result for many is that they also lost
the effectiveness which characterized their ministries in
the beginning.

Of course this is not true of every Bible College
or formal training institution. A few have maintained
faithfulness to their founding vision and are effectively
equipping leaders. If the church leadership does decide
to send the candidate for Bible College or seminary

training, it will be important for the local church to maintain close contact with the trainee during that period. Regular meetings with church leadership can provide needed encouragement, direction, and continued relationship with the trainee. Often leaders are negligent at this point and sometimes lose the missionary candidate to another group during the training period. Here again, the *sense of destiny* that is built into a church or organization will help retain leaders. It will also attract other leaders who may be looking for a challenge.

While in this phase of training, whether Bible College or a short-term training program, it is necessary for the trainee to begin developing a long-term strategy for the missionary work to which God is calling him. It will be important also for the local leadership to have input into this strategy. Everything possible should be done to help the trainee, from beginning to end, feel a vital connection to the sending church.

Effective cross-cultural training for missionary work is imperative. The sending group must not repeat the mistakes of some Western missions-sending organizations over the centuries by trying to import their own culture into the targeted group rather than letting the Gospel find its own cultural expressions. God's heart is that each people group will come to know Christ and that each of these groups will follow Him in the context of their mother culture. Some Western missionaries complicated the Gospel by teaching systems of belief, worship expressions, and even physical building models from their own culture rather than teaching the things that Jesus taught and permitting the culture in which they were working to find its own expressions of these things. This is what it means to plant *indigenous* churches. "He who has ears to hear, let him hear."

Missionaries must understand that people sometimes resist the Gospel because they feel it threatens their culture. Although they are tempted to believe the good news and receive Christ, they fear that they will be ostracized from their family or that, by accepting Christ, their entire culture will somehow be threatened. Sometimes this cannot be prevented because, to some extent, Jesus threatens every culture—at least the aspects of the culture which are not compatible with His teachings. However, in every society there are many cultural aspects which do not conflict with Jesus' teachings and should not be discarded but rather preserved and embraced. Missionaries, therefore, have a major responsibility to develop a deep understanding of and appreciation for the culture in which they are working and to insure that the Gospel is not presented in foreign cultural forms. We must remember that the goal of missionary work is to see people come to Jesus and to be formed into churches which are both biblically and culturally suitable.

4. THE APPRENTICE STAGE: (THREE MONTHS TO ONE YEAR)

An *apprentice* is a person who learns a skill or trade from someone who is an authority in that area. For centuries this was the primary way of training people for professions and often was very effective. Apprenticeship has much to offer those in ministry training as well. Any

classroom training must be supplemented with practical, "on-the-field" training. Working with a senior
missionary (preferably a *Strategy Coordinator*) who is
working among *Unreached Peoples* offers the candidate
essential and practical training and insight that can be
gained in no other way. The senior leadership of the
sending church should play a significant role in helping the trainee find suitable on-the-job training. This
may require networking with other ministries, but the
dividends will be well worth the effort. You may wish
to check the website www.churchplantingmovements.
com to see if you can locate a *Strategy Coordinator*
working near you.

5. The Mentor Stage:

Once the candidate has served with a missionary
mentor, he is ready to launch his own missionary ministry among the targeted people group. The strategy for
missionary church planting that he developed earlier
and revised after his practical field experience is now set
to be implemented. As he works among the new group
in cross-cultural ministry, and as the sending church or
organization trains other missionary candidates in the
future, they can send the new trainees to this person
(their own senior missionary) for mentoring instead of
sending him to gain the needed experience with other
groups. The missionary must remember that he is en-
deavoring to "work himself out of a job" with the unreached people group. Like Paul, he should normally
not plan to stay long-term among the group but rather

to train them properly and then move on to work with another unreached group.

This process needs to be repeated thousands of times over if we are to indeed finish *The Great Commission* in this generation. More churches and organizations must catch the vision for reaching the world's remaining 6,000+ unreached people groups and must be serious about completing *The Great Commission* in their own country first, and then reaching out to neighboring countries. They must be intentional about effectively training sufficient cross-cultural church planters to accomplish the goal. You may have an effective method of training missionaries already in place. If so, use your own and give God the glory. If not, please give serious thought to these suggestions.[6]

Sending Out Short-term Ministry Teams

As we contemplate sending trained workers into the harvest, thought should be given to the value of sending short-term missionary/church planting teams. Hundreds of churches and organizations around the world are using these short-term ministry teams in church planting, both among their own people groups and among *Unreached Peoples*. A church in Malaysia is using short-term teams very effectively. Almost every month this church sends out one or more teams to do evangelism, church planting, support ministry, or leadership training at home or abroad. These teams help their missionaries who are on the field, and they continue to fuel the vision for *The Great Commission* in the mother church.

This church finds there are numerous blessings which come as a result of sending out short-term teams.

First, the people who go out on these teams are great-ly blessed. In fact, as more people are sent, more mis-sionaries are called by God into full-time church plant-ing ministry from their church. One study I read some years ago stated that 80–90% of all missionaries serving on the field today received their call while serving on a short-term team.

Not only does this Malaysian church find that the people they send out are blessed, they find also that the mother church is blessed. As team members enlist prayer and financial support from church members, family, and friends, the people who agree to support them develop greater interest in the church's mission-ary outreach. Thus, the church, as it sends out more short-term teams, develops increased missionary vision and becomes more deeply committed to it. The Senior Pastor of this Malaysian church is a very wise man.

A wide variety of short-term teams can be sent out from a local church. They can send *fact-finding/research teams* which gather information on the group or village which is being targeted for church planting. They can send out *evangelistic teams* to witness and win people to Christ in the targeted area. They can send out *dis-cipleship teams* whose job is to help disciple the new believers or *leadership training teams* to help train the converts who have been identified as having leadership gifts. They may also send out *medical teams* to minister to the physical needs of people in the targeted village or ethnic group. Often doctors and nurses are willing to volunteer some of their time to reach out to a poor village or an unreached ethnic group.

These teams can be sent out for various lengths of

time—from a few days to a couple of weeks to a few months, depending on the mission they are to accomplish. All of this should be given careful consideration before the team leaves for the ministry assignment.

It is vital that short-term teams be adequately trained. Remember that churches which impact the world are churches which send *trained laborers* into the harvest. This training should have several components.

First, it should have *clear purpose and strategy.* If the team is to be successful, it must clearly understand its purpose and how that purpose will be carried out. The team should limit their focus to one particular people group or community for ministry.

Another essential component is *prayer.* Prayer is the key to everything. Long before leaving on the trip, team members should pray earnestly and specifically about situations they will face and the needs of the people to whom they are sent. Prayer should be done both individually and corporately. The church's intercessors should also focus on these needs.

The team must also be given good *skills training.* It will be vital to have proper and specific training for the particular assignment the team has been given. Qualified people must be enlisted to help train the team. If the team is a research team, they must be taught properly what information you want to gather and how to gather it. If they are an evangelistic team, they should be taught how to effectively evangelize.

An essential part of the preparation of these short-term teams is *attitude and behavioral training*. This may, in fact, be the most important of all, if the team is to be genuinely successful. Our success in Kingdom work will be deeply impacted by the attitudes manifested among the people to whom we are sent. Workers should be trained to have servant hearts and to exhibit attitudes of friendliness, compassion, humility, selflessness and consideration for others if they are to make a positive impact.

As a short-term missions trip is planned, consider carefully the goal of the team and provide the necessary training which will enable them to be successful. Plan for practical needs before the team leaves (materials, supplies, transportation, etc.). You will also need to develop a return strategy in order to preserve and direct the new enthusiasm of team members once they return and for processing information they have gathered.

To summarize, churches which effectively change their cultures and bring the Kingdom of God to their societies in a significant way are churches which send *trained laborers* into the harvest. They recognize the necessity of good leadership training and are committed not only to church planting outreach, but also to sending out workers who are qualified and skilled—those who can and will be effective in that outreach ministry.

Practical Application for Chapter 13

1. Would you say that your church is presently being effective in training qualified leaders and workers for cross-cultural ministry? If not, why not? If so, what are you presently doing that is yielding good results? How can that training be enlarged so that more quality workers can be trained?

2. Please review the two goals from this chapter that you were asked to set (10% of your members sent into evangelism and church planting ministry and 1% of your membership sent into full-time cross-cultural ministry). Have you done this already? If not, why not commit yourself to these goals now?

3. Review the five stages of effective training for cross-cultural ministry. Think about how you could incorporate these into the current training of your church.

4. Think about the Malaysian church which regularly sends short-term teams into outreach ministry. How can your church more effectively use short-term ministry teams to accomplish your goals for growth and expansion?

Endnotes

1   You will remember from chapter three that a missionary is "someone who enters another culture or ethnic group in order to make disciples."

2 My gratitude to Dr. Howard Foltz and his *Harvest Connection* teaching for insight in these areas.

3 Many indigenous church planting organizations are finding that non-formal processes of training of leaders, with adequate field experience and proper oversight, are being extremely effective in training some very capable missionary church planters.

4 *Breaking Tradition to Accomplish Vision* (Gupta and Lingenfelter), p. 23. Dr. Lingenfelter, Ph.D., serves as Professor and Provost and Senior Vice President at Fuller Theological Seminary in Pasadena, CA, USA.

5 Ibid, p. 17.

6 For a detailed study of how one ministry trained cross-cultural missionaries in India, see chapter four of *Breaking Tradition to Accomplish Vision*, Paul R. Gupta and Sherwood G. Lingenfelter, BMH Books, Winona Lake, IN, USA, 2006.

GIVING GENEROUSLY TO WORLD EVANGELIZATION

THE TENTH CHARACTERISTIC OF GREAT COMMISSION CHURCHES

"Give, and it will be given to you: good measure, pressed down, shaken together, and running over will be put into your bosom. For with the same measure that you use, it will be measured back to you."

(Luke 6:38)

The tenth characteristic of churches which impact the world is that they generously give to world evangelization. We have talked much about the needs of the world, about the unreached millions, and about the need to train and send tens of thousands of new church planters, especially in the 10/40 *Window,* in order to reach the more than 6,000 remaining people groups who have yet to hear. The question that remains is, "How are we going to finance such a global operation?" Where will the money come from to launch the needed missionaries and church planters into the ripened harvest fields of the world?

Churches in every culture that are helping to fulfill this *Great Commission* vision are churches which have discovered a vital secret. These churches are not looking to the West for money to reap the harvest which is at hand. Instead they are looking to God and to their own church members. They have grasped the importance of giving generously to the cause of world evangelization and are teaching it to their people. In so doing, they are being unusually blessed by God, just as He promised.

Examples of God's Blessing

A few years ago, my wife and I visited a church which was growing significantly in number but was having difficulties financially. They were in the process of raising money to acquire new church property and to build needed facilities but were having trouble doing so. As we presented the challenge of world evangelization, the congregation was deeply moved. They wanted to help, and to help significantly, but felt they did not have the resources to do so. So they took a step of faith. They made a *faith-promise.* As God would provide the money, they would commit to give a certain amount each month in order to help get the Gospel to those who have not heard. Several months later I spoke with the Pastor, and he told me that from the moment they made their commitment of faith, the regular income from their tithes and offerings had increased dramatically. In fact, their offerings had improved so significantly that they were able to acquire the property they needed and to build the new building. In addition, they doubled the amount they were giving for world evangelization.

This testimony is being repeated hundreds of times over in many parts of the world by both individuals and churches who are daring to believe God and who are willing to launch out in faith in their giving to help reach those who have not heard the Gospel. One such church in a key Asian city is now giving an amazing 70% of its total income to help finish *The Great Commission.* The Pastor told me that when God spoke to him about starting the church, He specifically told him to give away more than one-half of the income of the congregation to help reach the world for Christ. The Pastor obeyed. When the new church received its first offering, they set aside 51% of the amount received and put it in a separate fund for missionary outreach. That percentage has now increased gradually to its present level of 70%. According to the pastor's testimony, the money the church has left over for their own needs each month (the remaining 30% of their tithes and offerings) is more than sufficient to meet all of the needs of the congregation. How is this possible? It is possible because the congregation has both caught the vision for world evangelization and learned to give generously.

Self-supporting Churches

Churches on every continent and in every country must discover this truth for themselves if we are to make the kind of progress needed to finish the assignment Jesus gave us and if they are to experience the financial blessing of God upon their congregations. Earlier I mentioned the essential need for churches to be self-governing, self supporting, and self-propagating. It is essential that churches in each country look to God and to their own membership to provide the finances needed to evangelize, plant churches, support missionaries, train leaders, and build needed facilities. Majority World churches must not fall into the crippling trap of looking to the West to provide these funds. That tragic mistake has been made time and time again, seriously hampering the rapid progress of the Gospel. The result has been to create an attitude of dependency among many churches and groups around the world which has destroyed initiative, damaged faith, and stifled the work of God among them.

Two Suggested Financial Goals

At this point, I would like to challenge you with two financial goals for your congregation or group:

Goal #1: I want to suggest that your church begin *now* to commit at least 10% of your total church income to world evangelization. Put it in a special fund for evangelism and missions. I realize, for many groups, this will require a major step of faith. However, it is my belief that this should be the *minimal* goal of every *Great Commission Church*—and, as you make this commitment, God will honor your efforts and bless you in ways that you cannot now understand or imagine. Drastic times call for drastic actions, and if we are going to reach the two billion people who have yet to hear the Gospel, it will require sacrificial giving from God's people everywhere.

Goal #2: To regularly increase the percentage of total

finances given to world evangelization, as God blesses your congregation, until the church is giving at least 30% of its total income to help finish *The Great Commission* in this generation. This money can then be used for evangelism, church planting, and missions.

If more churches will make this kind of commitment (and I have every confidence they will), we will begin to see significant progress in our quest to finalize the mission assignment we have been given. Sacrifice is at the very heart of Jesus' message, and sacrifice we must if we are to finish the task.

The Matter of Tithing

Perhaps this is a good place to talk about the practice of tithing.[1] I am aware that this matter of giving to God and His Church is a subject on which there are many opinions. I am also aware that often those opinions are strongly held and that some will take issue with what I write here. Some people believe that tithing is clearly taught in the Scriptures (before the Old Testament Law was given, in the Law, and following the Law) and that it is a principle which should be practiced by all of God's people. Others believe that tithing was intended only for the Jewish people under the Old Testament Law, that it is not specifically taught in the New Testament, and therefore should not be taught as part of the New Covenant. My purpose here is not to do a biblical treatise on tithing, but rather to share a few thoughts on this vital subject. My personal opinion is that tithing is the most equitable way to support God's work in the world, the simplest to understand, the easiest to teach to God's people, and the method of giving which offers the most potential to raise the funds needed to help build God's Kingdom.

My wife and I have been consistent tithers for more than forty years. In fact, I do not believe that we have missed a single month of giving a tenth of our income to God since we were married. Would you like to know how we have done that—how we have *never* missed giving the tithe in forty years? The answer is simple. When we first became followers of Jesus, we began the practice of giving the tithe *first*. Before we bought food or paid any bills that were due, we gave to God, through our local congregation, one-tenth of our income for the support of His work. We have continued to do so each month from then until now. You may remember that God told Israel, when they harvested their crops, they were to bring the *first-fruits* of those crops as an offering to Him. One of the regular feasts which God instituted for the people of Israel was, in fact, called the *Feast of Firstfruits* (Exodus 23:16). God has never asked His people to give Him their leftovers. He consistently asks for our first and our best. Then He promises to bless us as we obey. Proverbs 3:9–10 says, "Honor the Lord with your possessions, And with the firstfruits of all your increase; So your barns will be filled with plenty, And your vats will overflow with new wine."

While I genuinely respect those who sincerely hold a different opinion about giving, in my more than forty years of ministry, I have never seen any systematic teaching on giving that has as much potential, is as easy to understand, or consistently raises as much money for the Kingdom as tithing, when it is taught clearly, consistently, and passionately. If I were a pastor in any part of the world, I would teach all of God's people under my care to be consistent tithers. Regardless of what one thinks about tithing, it cannot be disputed that God has promised to abundantly bless those who give and to bless them in *proportion* to their giving (See Proverbs 11:24; Luke 6:38; 2 Corinthians 9:6). To promote giving in any way which results in people giving less rather than more is to do both them and God's Church a disservice. If anyone wants to teach another method of giving to God's people, he should be sure that it is consistent with Scripture, that it is taught clearly, systematically, and passionately, and that it results in believers giving liberally and consistently to the work of God.

Faith Promise Giving

Having said that, I must add that even if all of God's people tithe (especially in the Majority World), it will likely not produce enough money to finance the massive church planting effort which must be launched across North Africa, the Middle East, and Asia in order to reach the masses who have not heard. More finances will be needed. Where will these additional funds come from? There is a concept which the Holy Spirit appears to be advancing across much of the Body of Christ around the world—one which is being used in hundreds of churches on every continent, to raise significant money for world evangelization. The idea is often referred to as *Faith Promise Giving* and is one which offers tremendous potential for the adequate funding of world evangelization, particularly among countries of the Two-Thirds World.

In Genesis 12, God made two great promises to

Abraham. If Abraham would obey Him and follow His direction, God said that He would, first of all, bless Abraham in a significant way. Abraham would be given descendants like the stars of the heavens and the sands of the seashore. God would, in fact, make him a *Father of Nations.* He would also be given a land which God would show him as an everlasting possession. Secondly, God promised to make Abraham a blessing to others. Through Abraham, in fact, all the families of the earth would be blessed. Most scholars have concluded that this second blessing included, among other things, the promise that Messiah would one day be born from Abraham's offspring and bring a new inward righteousness to God's people together with an ability to know God personally and intimately. As we know, both of those promises did come to pass. Abraham became one of the most prosperous and renowned men of his day. Nations came from his loins, and the world was blessed beyond understanding when Jesus Christ of Nazareth, the Messiah, was born from Abraham's descendants (Matthew 1:1).

In the New Testament, Paul explains God's blessing upon Abraham further when he makes the rather astonishing statement that every true believer in Christ is a son of Abraham and an heir according to the promise (Galatians 3:29). What is the promise to which Paul refers? He is, of course, speaking of the two-fold promise given to Abraham—that Abraham would be blessed and that he would be a blessing. Let's not miss the implications. God is implicitly stating His desire to bless His people everywhere—in every country and among every people group—and to make them a blessing to others around them. The goodness of God is shown in a remarkable way as He sets forth His desire to shower His favor, both physically and spiritually, upon all of the people groups in the world through Abraham and his descendants.

Although much has been written and spoken, especially during the past few decades, that has taken the truth of God's prosperity to an extreme, we must never lose sight of the fact that the essential promise stands. God may not desire that each person be as wealthy and famous as Abraham, but He does want them to be blessed in both of these ways. That fact cannot be denied. God is a good God who delights to shower His favor upon His children everywhere. He gets no glory from poverty, or want, or indigence, or hunger, or insignificance. The particular point I desire to make is that through *Faith Promise Giving* (and other ideas like it), God often reveals His goodness to His people. As He teaches them to give, He honors their giving and both blesses them and makes them a blessing to the world around them.

What Faith Promise Giving Is

What is this *Faith Promise Giving* idea that God is using to build His Kingdom around the world and that offers such potential for helping to fund *The Great Commission? Faith Promise Giving* is primarily three things:

- First, it is an amount of money, in addition to the tithe, which a believer trusts God to provide through him each month so that he can give specifically for the cause of world evangelization. In systematically giving the money through his own church or organization, the believer can help to send new laborers into Kingdom work to reach those who have not heard.

- Second, it is a step of *faith* that God will provide in some special way the money each month so that one can give it. This a *faith* promise. Even though the believer may not have money to give, he specifically asks God to provide it and trusts Him to do so. Usually a *faith promise* is made for a one-year period after which time the entire process will be reevaluated and renewed by the individual.

- Third, it is a *promise* to God that, as He provides the money, the believer will not use it for himself or his family but that he will give it so that new missionaries and church planters can be sent out to reach those who have not heard.

What Faith Promise Giving Is Not

Now that we have seen what *Faith Promise Giving* is, for the sake of clear understanding, let me suggest five things that it is *not:*

- First, *Faith Promise Giving* is *not* giving the tithe—it is in *addition* to the tithe. In many churches and organizations, the *tithe* from believers goes to finance normal operations of the church (salaries of workers, evangelism, discipling of converts, leadership training, upkeep on church properties, etc.). Money from *Faith Promise Giving* should be designated specifically for church planting in unreached towns and villages and among *Unreached Peoples* and should not be used by the church for salaries or for operating expenses.

- Second, the *Faith Promise* is not based on money you currently have. If your situation is like mine, even though you would like to give so that other workers can go, you may not have any excess money at the end of the month to give for this cause. For my family, it takes all we have to live. After giving the *tithe* to God each month, my wife and I for years did not have anything left over to give for world evangelization. The *Faith Promise* gave us a good way to believe God for *additional* money to give for helping to finance the end-time harvest. It can do the same for you.

- Third, *Faith Promise Giving* is not exercising faith in order to *get* something from God. Rather it is using the faith God has given us to be able to *give* more to God and His Kingdom. It is not a selfish exercise or an attempt to manipulate God. It is an unselfish exercise designed to raise needed funds to help finish *The Great Commission.*

- Fourth, it is not some kind of *pledge* or *vow* that we make and are *required* to pay each month. No one should ask the individual about his *Faith Promise* because no one else need know about it. This is simply a faith matter between the individual and God. As God provides the money, he gives it. If God does not provide, he cannot give it.

- Fifth, the *Faith Promise* should not be some kind of foolish commitment that one makes. The idea is not that a believer will make a promise to give some excessive amount of money to world evangelization each month. Rather the amount one chooses to trust God for should be in harmony with his current level of faith and should be based on what he senses God to be saying to him in the matter.

Principles of Faith Promise Giving

Now, it will be helpful to describe *Faith Promise Giving* by listing five foundational principles upon which the concept is built:

1. The *Faith Promise* is one way of producing *new wealth* in order to help finish *The Great Commission.* One of the insights God gave to Israel through Moses in the Old Testament had to do with this issue: "But remember the Lord your God, for it is He who gives you the *ability to produce wealth,* and so *confirms his covenant,* which He swore to your forefathers, as it is today" (Deuteronomy 8:18, NIV, italics added). In order to obtain the needed funds for world evangelization, we must have new ways to produce them. In this passage God promises Israel that, as they followed Him and obeyed His commands, He would give them the ability to produce wealth. God said this would be one way that He would confirm that they were in covenant with Him. *Faith Promise Giving* may be one of the ways that God is giving His children, especially in the Two-Thirds World, the capability of producing the new wealth needed to complete *The Great Commission.* It may also be one of the ways He confirms that He is in covenant with His people and that His blessings are upon their lives.

In the New Testament, Paul said of the Macedonian believers, "For I testify that they gave as much as they were able, and even beyond their ability" (2 Corinthians 8:3, NIV). We might ask, "How can people give more than they are able to give?" *Faith Promise Giving* certainly seems to be one way in which this can be done. It is giving more than one has the ability to give, by trusting God to provide additional money to be given.

2. The *Faith Promise* is a way that *everyone* can participate in giving for world evangelization, even the poor. Paul goes on to say of the believers in Macedonia that, "Out of the most severe trial, their overflowing joy and their extreme poverty welled up in rich generosity" (2 Corinthians 8:2, NIV). These God-followers did not give only when they had excess money, but they gave also when they were under acute testing. Out of great scarcity they were able to give in order to meet the need at hand—to help the impoverished believers in Judea. Through *Faith Promise Giving,* believers in every part of the world, even those who are experiencing hardship and lack themselves, can give to the great need at hand which is to help send workers to reach those who have not heard.

3. The *Faith Promise* is one way that God can bless His people financially. In 2 Corinthians 9:6, Paul reminds us of a significant truth when he says, "Remember this: whoever sows sparingly will also reap sparingly, and whoever sows generously will also reap generously" (NIV). All of God's people in every country desire to be blessed by Him. No one enjoys living in poverty and want. Scripture is very clear that one of the ways

we receive financial blessings is by giving. Paul says plainly in this passage that reaping God's blessings is directly proportional to our giving. If we give little, we receive little. If we give much, we reap much. This is God's promise.

Jesus introduced this subject in the New Testament when He said, "Give, and it will be given to you: good measure, pressed down, shaken together, and running over will be poured into your bosom. For with the same measure you use, it will be measured back to you" (Luke 6:38). The truth is obvious: we receive from God according to the measure of our giving. Through *Faith Promise Giving,* we are able to give to God in greater measure than we could otherwise and, therefore, can expect to receive from Him in similar measure. So, not only will we able to give more for world evangelization, our families will also be blessed in return.

4. The *Faith Promise* should be given cheerfully and without pressure. As Paul discussed giving with the Macedonian believers, he told them: "Each man should give what he has decided in his heart to give, not reluctantly or under compulsion, for God loves a *cheerful* giver" (2 Corinthians 9:7). No person should give the *Faith Promise* (or anything else for that matter) because they feel pressured to give. Giving, according to God, is to be a matter of the heart so that it can be done with joy. Each month, my wife and I give a *Faith Promise* (in addition to the tithe) in order to help other workers reach those who have not heard—and we do so joyfully, with a smile on our faces. That's the way giving was intended to be done. Heavy-handed

pressure placed on people to give has no place in the Kingdom.

5. Before we give our *Faith Promise* to God, we should first give ourselves to Him. Again, Paul says of the believers in Macedonia, "They urgently pleaded with us for the privilege of sharing...but they gave themselves first to the Lord and then to us in keeping with God's will" (2 Corinthians 8:4,5). Can you imagine people *urgently pleading* for the opportunity to give? That statement tells us something of the quality of life that was in those Macedonian believers. I know many pastors who would love to have a congregation like that! The important thing to note is that they first gave *themselves* to the Lord and to His service before giving their money. They did not use their giving, as some Christians in the West do, as a way of easing their consciences so that they would not have to get involved personally in the work of the Kingdom. The Macedonian followers of Jesus were committed— heart, mind, and body—to participate in God's work in the world.

A Personal Challenge

Now that *Faith Promise Giving* is clearly defined, here is a question: What finances will *your* faith release for God's Kingdom? What does God want *you* to believe Him for so that more workers can go to plant churches in the thousands of unreached towns and villages of the world? What *Faith Promise* does God want *you* to make?

It should be noted that, in order for *Faith Promise Giving* to work effectively, the entire church or group should be given the opportunity to trust God in this way. The concept should be clearly taught and applied—without pressure of any kind. In fact, I have found it effective to have a *Faith Promise Sunday* when the pastor preaches or teaches on this subject.[2] At the close of the message, each person may be given a form on which to make his *Faith Promise* if he so desires. There should be no place for the individual to sign.[3] No one need know whether a person is giving a *Faith Promise* or not. It is simply a matter between the individual and God. It is fine to collect the faith promises and total the amounts in order to have an idea of how much money to expect, but no one should know who participates and who does not.

One good plan of action might be for the pastor or the key leaders of the group to try making a *Faith Promise* first—in order to prove among themselves that it truly works. Then they can preach and teach the concept with authority and conviction to the entire church. For a number of years my wife and I have trusted God to provide money each month for our *Faith Promise.* We can tell you that God has always provided the money for us every month—and we live by faith, trusting God to provide our income, just as many of God's servants do throughout the Two-Thirds World.

Faith Promise Giving is not an infallible plan, but it is a good plan that God is using all over the world to provide needed money for world evangelization. I have seen no better plan anywhere for raising the large amounts of money needed to help finish *The Great Commission.* Why not try it?

Practical Application for Chapter 14

1. Please review the two financial goals you were asked to set at the beginning of the chapter. If you have not already set such goals for your congregation, why not pray about setting them now?

2. Review what was discussed in the chapter concerning *tithing*. Are you a tither? If not, why not? Do you regularly teach the people in your church or group to tithe? If not, why not? If so, have they begun to put it into practice? You may be doing them a tremendous disservice by not teaching them to give regularly and systematically.

3. Pray about making a *Faith Promise* yourself—before teaching this subject to anyone else. Ask God if He wants you to do this. If He does, ask Him how much He wants you to trust Him for each month—so that you personally can give to the cause of world evangelization. Try it for a few months to see if it works.

4. Once you have proven that *Faith Promise Giving* works in your life, develop a plan for teaching the concept to your entire church or group. This is an outstanding way to raise money to help support workers from your church who will be missionaries to *Unreached Peoples* and who will do church planting in unreached towns and villages of your province or state.

Endnotes

1   The word *tithe* means "tenth." For centuries God's people around the world have practiced the regular giving of the *tithe*—one-tenth of their total income (wages, crops, etc.) in order to help finance the work of God's Kingdom.

2   For the concept to work the best, the pastor should preach and teach on the subject for several weeks in order to help the people clearly understand. They should be told clearly what the money is to go for (sending out workers to unreached peoples and villages) and how to participate.

3   See the Appendix for a sample *Faith Promise* form.

TOGETHER WE CAN FINISH THE GREAT COMMISSION

"And this gospel of the kingdom will be preached in all the world as a witness to all the nations, and then the end will come."

(Matthew 24:14)

As stated at the outset, the primary purpose of this book is to help God's people around the world gain new vision, more passion, greater determination, and clearer strategy for finishing *The Great Commission* in this generation—and to impact the world around us in the process. I am aware that God's people in past generations have also made similar calls and challenges. Although significant progress has been made during the past few centuries in reaching the world's 16,000 people groups, the job is by no means finished. Much remains to be done. However, the completion of the assignment may be coming into view on the distant horizon. Dr. Peter Wagner's statement that, *for the first time in history,* the church of Jesus Christ now has a realistic chance to finish *The Great Commission,* may indeed be true. There are several reasons why it may be possible to complete the task in this generation when it was not possible in past generations. Remember that we have already stated that although it is difficult, if not impossible, to know exactly when and how *The Great Commission* will be fulfilled, our goal must be to see a *Church Planting Movement* among each people group on earth

Dr. Ralph Winter reminds us that in 1974 the Christian world was stunned to discover that 75% of the world's non-believers were, at that point, beyond the reach of same-culture evangelism. That number has been reduced significantly over the past few decades. Today approximately one-third of non-believers live within *Unreached Peoples* and that number is shrinking.

In my opinion there are at least nine significant *acts of God* which are now converging in the earth to enable the Church of Jesus Christ to finish its divine mandate. It is not my intention to comment largely on these nine factors, but to make a few brief comments about each. These God-acts are as follows and are in no certain order of significance:

The global prayer movement has mobilized millions of Christians around the world to pray for world evangelization and is without question the largest prayer movement in the history of the world. This revival of prayer that has been taking place over the past couple of decades is providing the impetus for finishing *The Great Commission.* The "Praying through the Window" effort, for example, mobilized more than 40 million followers of Jesus to intercede for specific *Unreached Peoples* in the 10/40 *Window.*

Current prayer emphases such as the *Global Day of Prayer* are also contributing extensively to this effort. Graham Power, Chairman of *Global Day of Prayer,* reports that on June 4, 2006, the emphasis brought together 400–500 million people in 198 countries of the world to pray for the evangelization of their countries. This was the largest gathering of God's people for prayer in history. Publications such as *The Global Prayer Digest* (www.global-prayer-digest.com) and plans like the *Harvest-Linked Prayer Initiative* (www.ethne.net) are also helping to mobilize the Church of Jesus Christ to pray for the world's unreached millions.

The specific targeting of the world's *Unreached Peoples* has pinpointed where the primary remaining work needs to be done. Only recently has the research been available to help us see more clearly what it will take to finish the task. Until the Lausanne Congress on World Evangelization in 1974, most of the world's missions focus was on nation-states. Afterward, the missions community was able to see more plainly the "hidden peoples" who must be reached with the Gospel. Ministries such as *Joshua Project* and publications such as *Operation World* and *The World Christian Encyclopedia,* along with many other organizations and publications both in the USA and in the Two-Thirds World, have contributed immeasurably to this emphasis. It is encouraging to note that during the past 20 years there has been more than a 250% increase in the number of missionaries who are focusing on *Unreached Peoples.* COMIBAM, for example, now has 14% of their missionary force focusing on the unreached and the Church in Singapore has an estimated 25% of missionaries concentrating on *Unreached Peoples.*[1]

The emergence of the burgeoning missionary movement of the Majority World is now surpassing the West in the number of missionaries being sent out. This movement is rapidly developing the vision, the commitment, and the resources to make a colossal impact on the unfinished task. This is one of the primary ingredients missing from efforts to finish *The Great Commission* in past generations.

Dr. Ralph Winter informs us that in the 10 years which followed the launching of COMIBAM in Latin America, the Latin Americans founded 400 missions agencies and sent out 4,000 new missionaries to five continents. This is characteristic of what is now happening throughout the Majority World. Christianity Today reported in 1973 that there were 3,411 non-Western missionaries in the world. Today, although it is difficult to number them with accuracy, there are well over 100,000 missionaries from the Two-Thirds World.[2]

Scott Moreau, Chair of Intercultural Studies at Wheaton College (Wheaton, Illinois, USA) says, "The day of Western missionary dominance is over, not because Western Missions have died, but because the rest of the world has caught the vision and is engaged and energized."[3] The Church in South Korea is a prime example of this. At the time of this writing, the Korean

Church has sent out 13,000 missionaries and is currently sending them out at a rate of 1,100 per year. The Koreans have become the second largest missionary sending church after the USA. A goal of sending 100,000 full-time Korean missionaries by the year 2030 has been set by the Korea World Mission Association (KWMA). On the continent of Africa, the Church in Nigeria is leading the way, having sent out more than 5,000 missionaries who are serving in 56 countries. Currently there are more than 4,000 mission agencies in the Majority World and many of them are focusing the zeal that is so characteristic of majority world churches on *Unreached Peoples.*

The extraordinary Pentecostal/charismatic explosion that has occurred over the past century has birthed hundreds of thousands of new churches, both in the West and in the Two-Thirds World. According to charismatic historian Dr. Vinson Synan, this movement now has more than 600 million constituents and has created approximately one million new churches during the past century. This phenomenon has significantly contributed to the gathering of a potential army of dedicated missionary church planters in the Majority World which will largely provide the manpower for completing the task of world evangelization. During the latter half of the past century three gigantic, world-wide missionary organizations were formed which have sent tens of thousands of missionaries into the world: *Youth With A Mission, Operation Mobilization,* and *Campus Crusade for Christ.* At present the Pentecostal movement is growing at 58% per year.[4]

The re-emergence of *power evangelism* (signs, wonders, healings, and miracles) on a massive scale has accompanied this world-wide charismatic movement and has resulted in millions of lost people coming to Christ. The work of God is progressing more rapidly than perhaps at any point in church history. On every continent and in almost every country of the world, God is at work, revealing Himself in power and authority through signs and wonders. As we have already noted, it is estimated that 70% of all conversions taking place in the Two-Thirds World today are the result of signs and wonders.

The technological explosion of the past few decades has added enormous volumes of easily-accessible information, combined with high-speed communication, to the arsenal of tools available for the end-time harvest. Exploding computer technology, as well as radio broadcasts and telecasts that are heard and seen daily in many parts of the world, makes the Gospel increasingly available throughout the earth. It is more and more evident that computer assisted communication and information sharing through modems and networks is changing the way we do missions and has enormous potential to help us do our job better and faster.

Fast and affordable travel has contributed significantly to the globalization of the world and has revolutionized world missions. Now one can travel from his home to almost any part of the world in under thirty hours. This has brought short-term missions to the forefront of missions strategy and has resulted in tens of thousands of short-term missionaries and missionary teams being sent into the missions arena both from the West and from the countries of the Two-Thirds World. One may debate the real and lasting contribution of some of these individuals and teams, but it cannot be debated that it has brought many more players onto the field. Without question some of these new players are helping to make a significant difference in getting the Gospel to those who have not heard. Another positive result is that many more local churches are now becoming more directly involved in and passionate about the missionary task.

The birth of *Church Planting Movements* on every continent is enabling the Church of Jesus Christ to impact the world's *Unreached Peoples* far more quickly and with much greater effectiveness than ever imagined. This has been sufficiently discussed in earlier chapters but is one of the major *acts of God* which is significantly contributing to the finishing of *The Great Commission*. These *Church Planting Movements* are indicative of a renewed emphasis on evangelism and church planting which has come to the Body of Christ in the past few decades. The result is that currently more than 100,000 new Christians are being added to the Kingdom every day and more than 4,500 new congregations are started each week.[5]

The translation of Scripture into the world's languages is helping immensely to finish the task. At least part of the Bible is now available in 2,403 of the world's 6,912 languages. According to Wycliffe Bible Translators, translation is now in progress for another 1,640 languages. According to Wikipedia, the Bible is now available in whole or in part to 98% of the world's population in a language in which they are fluent.[6]

Although Avery Willis, Executive Director of International Orality Network (ION),[7] informs us that 70% of the world's population can't, don't, and won't read and that four billion people are "oral learners," this major gap is also in the process of being filled. The advent of the *Jesus Film*,[8] which has reportedly had more than six billion viewings and resulted in 201 million decisions for Christ, along with several other significant visual and oral evangelism tools and efforts, are giving a greater percentage of the world's least-reached peoples access to the Gospel.[9] Willis informs us that the world of missions is now waking up to the fact that the reaching of oral learners with the Gospel is fundamental to completing *The Great Commission,* and that significant steps are currently being taken to meet this need.

The convergence of these nine factors leads me to conclude that the end may indeed, for the first time in history, genuinely be in sight. *Great Commission Believers* and *Great Commission Churches* are emerging in larger numbers all over the world. As they awaken with fresh vision, greater passion, clearer strategy, deeper commitment, increased unity, and enhanced perseverance, the Body of Christ may well be able to complete in this generation what it has not been able to accomplish during the past 2,000 years. As this happens, we could well see the return of Jesus Christ of Nazareth as King of Kings and Lord of Lords and see His Kingdom established on earth in its fullness. Even so, come, Lord Jesus. Amen.

Practical Application for Chapter 15

1. Review the above nine factors which are contributing significantly to the *finishing* of *The Great Commission*. Which one or two of these caught your attention the most and why?

2. Can you think of any other factors which are significantly contributing to this effort of seeing *The Great Commission* completed? If so, what are they and what contribution are they making?

3. What role are you going to have in helping to finish *The Great Commission?* Please make this a significant matter of prayer. Ask God to ignite a fire inside you to help see this mandate from Jesus completed in this generation. Ask Him what He wants you to do in response to reading this book.

Endnotes

1 "Where We Are." *Momentum* magazine. March/April 2006 issue. p. 29 (www.momentum-mag.org).

2 Christianity Today Online Magazine. March, 2006. Article entitled, "Missions Incredible."

3 Ibid.

4 *Momentum* magazine. March/April, 2006, p. 31.

5 "Where We Are." Momentum magazine. March/April 2006. p. 30.

6 www.wikipedia.org

7 International Orality Network is a partnership of 22 mission agencies including the Southern Baptist Convention's International Mission Board (IMB), Youth With a Mission (YWAM), Trans World Radio, Campus Crusade for Christ, and Wycliffe Bible Translators.

8 The *Jesus Film*, according to their website, is now available in 947 languages and has 16,653 film prints and more than 42,000,000 videocassettes, DVD's, and VCD's in circulation.

9 See www.oralbible.com and www.vernacularmedia. org

A FINAL CHALLENGE

"So Jesus said to them again, 'Peace to you! As the Father has sent Me, I also send you.'"

(John 20:21)

In conclusion, I want to ask a few questions of you personally. What do you plan to do with the remainder of your life? How will you invest your future—in something insignificant and self-serving or in something which truly matters? How will your life make a difference in the world? Every person is born with a song to sing, but, as Oliver Wendell Holmes once said, "Most people go to their graves with their music still inside them." What did he mean by that? He meant that most people live their entire lives and die without ever discovering the reason for which they were born. How tragic. The real question is, "What about you?" Have you discovered the reason why you were born? If so, will you sing your song? If not, will you put forth the faith and effort to find out what that song is—or will you be like one of the world's untold millions who die without ever discovering your purpose in life?

From cover to cover the Bible teaches that every

person is born for a reason. There are no accidental births in this world. God affirms that He is at work in the life of each person, even while they are being formed in their mother's womb (Psalm 139:13–18). This, of course, includes you. God has put destiny in the heart of every person and part of that destiny, for followers of Jesus, has to do with carrying out His final mandate to us. It is unthinkable that we would be one of Jesus' disciples and not do something significant to help carry out His final command. So what will your role be? Do you have a vision for your part in seeing *The Great Commission* fulfilled?

It is my personal conviction that people who want to impact their world for Christ need a vision that is all-consuming—a vision that is worthy of their life— a vision that is worth dying for. Dan Erickson once said, "I don't fear failure. I fear succeeding at something which really doesn't matter. Most men are succeeding in matters that don't really matter." Please give this some serious thought. Ask God what role He wants you to play in finishing *The Great Commission* in this generation. As you come to understand what it is, give yourself fully to it. Give God everything in your life— your time, your talent, your abilities, your family, your money, your future—everything.

Please read the *Angel Stadium Declaration* which follows and join with multitudes of Jesus-followers around the world who are surrendering everything to Christ and who are participating with Him in the spread of His Kingdom throughout the earth. This dec- laration is in reality a prayer—a serious prayer of com- mitment of one's entire life to Christ. Please consider praying this prayer with sincerity and conviction. Then follow through with that commitment and you will learn what it is to truly live.

"He is no fool who gives what he cannot keep to gain what he cannot lose."

...Missionary Martyr Jim Elliott

The Angel Stadium Declaration
April 17, 2005

Note: On April 17, more than 30,000 members of the Saddleback Church gathered in Angel Stadium in California to celebrate the congregation's 25th anniversary. At the end of the celebration, everyone stood together to read the declaration below. May every person who reads this book join in the spirit of this commitment as we set our faces steadfastly toward the goal of finishing *The Great Commission.*

Today I am stepping across the line. I'm tired of waffling, and I'm finished with wavering. I've made my choice; the verdict is in; and my decision is irrevocable. I'm going God's way. There's no turning back now!

I will live the rest of my life serving God's purposes with God's people on God's planet for God's glory. I will use my life to celebrate his presence, cultivate his character, participate in his family, demonstrate his love, and communicate his Word.

Since my past has been forgiven, and I have a purpose for living and a home awaiting in heaven, I refuse to waste any more time or energy on shallow living, petty thinking, trivial talking, thoughtless doing, useless regretting, hurtful resenting, or faithless worrying.

Instead I will magnify God, grow to maturity, serve in ministry, and fulfill my mission in the membership of his family.

Because this life is preparation for the next, I will value worship over wealth, "we" over "me," character over comfort, service over status, and people over possessions, position, and pleasures. I know what matters most and I'll give it all I've got. I'll do the best I can with what I have for Jesus Christ today.

I won't be captivated by culture, manipulated by critics, motivated by praise, frustrated by problems, debilitated by temptation, or intimidated by the devil. I'll keep running my race with my eyes on the goal, not the sidelines or those running by me. When times get tough and I get tired, I won't back up, back off, back down, back out, or backslide. I'll just keep moving forward by God's grace. I'm Spirit-led, purpose-driven, and mission-focused, so I cannot be bought, I will not be compromised, and I shall not quit until I finish the race.

I'm a trophy of God's amazing grace so I will be gracious to everyone, grateful for everyday, and generous with everything that God entrusts to me.

To my Lord and Savior Jesus Christ, I say: *However, whenever, wherever, and whatever* you ask me to do, my answer in advance is yes! Wherever you lead and whatever the cost, I'm ready. Anytime. Anywhere. Anyway. *Whatever it takes Lord; whatever it takes!* I want to be used by you in such a way that on that final day I'll hear you say, "Well done, thou good and faithful one. Come on in, and let the eternal party begin!"[1]

ENDNOTE

1 This article is printed from the website www.
   PurposeDriven.com. Copyright 2005 by Rick Warren.
   Used by permission. All rights reserved

HERE I AM, LORD

written by Dan Schutte

I, the Lord of sea and sky,
I have heard My people cry
All who dwell in dark and sin,

My hand will save,
I who made the stars of night
I will make their darkness bright
Who will bear my light to them,
Whom shall I send?

Here I am, Lord, Is it I, Lord?
I have heard You calling in the night
I will go, Lord, if You lead me
I will hold Your people in my heart.

I'm the Lord of wind and flame
I will tend the poor and lame
I will set a feast for them,
My hand will save

Finest bread I will provide
Till their hearts be satisfied
I will give my life to them,
Whom shall I send?

Here I am, Lord, Is it I, Lord?
I have heard You calling in the night
I will go, Lord, if You lead me
I will hold Your people in my heart.

APPENDIX

Note 1: It is noteworthy that the term "church" is used only a few times in the New Testament while the term "kingdom" is used nearly 100 times. Through the ages the Church of Jesus Christ has often been slowed down by institutionalization and has lost sight of its responsibility to preach, pray, and labor for the coming of God's Kingdom into the societies of the earth. The "Good News" that Jesus introduced to the world was not simply an individualistic message. Rather it was a message that would impact the world at the deepest level and bring righteousness, justice, peace, hope and joy to all (Romans 14:17). Jesus' goal was to revolutionize society so that each person and family might enjoy the benefits of His Kingdom. Followers of Jesus in every part of the world need to understand this and not simply seek to produce new believers and churches, but to make those believers and churches instruments of the Kingdom. We must understand the need to bring a *holistic* message which offers hope to people everywhere who are held captive by sickness, oppression, poverty, and sin of every nature.

Note 2: There is a real sense in which every Christian is called by God. Such passages as Romans 8:28–30, Romans 11:29, 1 Corinthians 1:26–29, 1 Corinthians 7:20, and Ephesians 2:10 reveal this clearly. As a child who was reared in church, I was aware early that people were *called* by God to do things. But, for the most part, there were only three classes of people which made up "the called"—pastors, evangelists, and missionaries. These were shown to be the really important people in the world. These were the ones who carried out the real work of the Kingdom. Everyone else was, more or less, on the sidelines. Apostles and prophets were almost totally ignored. However, when I began to study the Scriptures for myself, I came to see that every believer is called by God. The church is like a human body. One is like an eye, one like a hand, one like a foot, and one like a liver. Some are more visible than others but each is important. Each has an essential job to do. If any of the jobs are not done (if any of the parts of the Body are not functioning), then the Body is left in a crippled state of some kind.

One of the greatest needs today is for pastors and leaders to understand that each person in their congregations is both gifted and called. They also must come to see that one of their primary responsibilities as a leader is to help the members identify those gifting and callings and to equip them to participate with them in ministry. Such an idea has the potential to totally revolutionize a church and to transform it from an ordinary church to a *Great Commission Church.*

Note 3: The Saddleback Vision (shared by Pastor Rick Warren on March 30, 1980)[1]

It is the dream of a place where the hurting, the depressed, the frustrated, and the confused can find love, acceptance, help, hope, forgiveness, guidance, and encouragement.

It is the dream of sharing the Good News of Jesus Christ with the hundreds of thousands of residents in south Orange County.

It is the dream of welcoming 20,000 members into the fellowship of our church family—loving, learning, laughing, and living in harmony together.

It is the dream of developing people to spiritual maturity through Bible studies, small groups, seminars, retreats, and a Bible school for our members.

It is the dream of equipping every believer for a significant ministry by helping them discover the gifts and talents God gave them.

It is the dream of sending out hundreds of career missionaries and church workers all around the world, and empowering every member for a personal life mission in the world. It is the dream of sending our members by the thousands on short-term missions projects to every continent. It is the dream of starting at least one new daughter church every year.

It is the dream of at least 50 acres of land, on which will be built a regional church for south Orange County—with beautiful, yet simple, facilities including a worship center seating thousands, a counseling and prayer center, classrooms for Bible studies and training lay ministers, and a recreation area. All of this will be designed to minister to the total person—spiritually, emotionally, physically, and socially—and set in a peaceful, inspiring garden landscape.

I stand before you today and state in confident assurance that these dreams will become reality. Why? Because they are inspired by God.

Note 4: In his book *Church Planting Movements,* author David Garrison shares six lessons used by John & Hope Chen for training converts in China.[2] The six lessons are as follows:

Lesson One: Assurance of Salvation

- The new believer's new relationship to God in Christ is reconfirmed through Scripture.

- Key verses to review and memorize: Isaiah 59:2; Ephesians 2:8–9; 1 Peter 3:18; John 10:28; 2 Corinthians 5:17; 1 John 1:9; 1 John 5:13.

- The trainer helps the new believer create a "New Birth Certificate" to keep in his or her Bible. It states the date when "I received Jesus into my heart as my Savior. He forgave my sin, became my Lord and took control of my life. Now I have become a child of God and a new creation." Signed_____.

Lesson Two: A Life of Prayer

- The trainer explains why we need to pray, the content

of prayer, three types of answers to prayer, and new attitudes that result from prayer.

- Why we need to pray: Luke 18:1; Ephesians 6:18; 1 Peter 5:7; Jeremiah 33:3; Hebrews 4:16; Philippians 4:6–7.

- The content of prayer: 1 John 1:9; Philippians 4:6–7; Psalm 135:3; 1 Thessalonians 5:18; 1 Timothy 2:1

- Three answers to prayer—Yes, No, Wait

- New attitudes resulting from prayer—James 1:6; James 4:2–3; Psalm 66:18; 1 John 5:14; Luke 18:1.

Lesson Three: Having a Daily Quiet Time

- The trainer explains: "If we really want to know God, we need to have close regular contact with Him." Set a regular time for daily quiet time with God.

- What can we learn about devotional time with God from these biblical examples? Genesis 19:27; Psalm 5:3; Daniel 6:10; Mark 1:35; Psalm 42:1–2; Psalm 119:147–148

- Suggested tools for quiet time: Bible, pen, and notebook, quiet place, set time, a reading plan.

- Preparation for quiet time: Psalm 119:18

Lesson Four: Understanding and Being Church

- Church is not a building, but "the household of the living God" (1 Timothy 3:15). Church consists of God's people and can meet in your own home.

- What do these verses teach us about church? Romans 12:5; Ephesians 1:23; Ephesians 5:23.

- The church has five purposes: Worship—Psalm 149:1; Fellowship—Hebrews 10:25; Teaching—Matthew 28:20; Evangelism—Acts 1:8; and Ministry—Matthew 22:26–30; Romans 12:9–13.

- The church has rights and obligations: Baptism—Matthew 3:15; Romans 6:3–4; The Lord's Supper—Matthew 26:26–30; Tithes and Offerings—Leviticus 27:30–31.

Lesson Five: Knowing God

- God, as revealed in Jesus Christ, may be radically different from the conceptions of God that the new believer held in his or her previous life. Understanding God is a lifelong pursuit, but a good foundation begins here.

- What can we learn about the nature of God from these passages? Jeremiah 31:3; Ephesians 2:4–5; 1 John 3:1; Luke 15:11–24; 2 Thessalonians 3:3; 2 Kings 6:15–18; Daniel 3; 1 Corinthians 10:13; Philippians 4:19;

Matthew 6:31–32; Romans 8:31–39; Hebrews 12:6–7; 2 Timothy 3:16; 1 John 4:4.

Lesson Six: God's Will for You

- At this point the training has come full circle. While the new believer is incorporated into a POUCH church meeting in a home[3] POUCH is an acronym for

    P - Participative Bible Study;

    O - Obedience as the mark of success for every believer and church;

    U - Unpaid and multiple leaders in each church;

    C - Cell groups of 10–20 believers meeting in each group;

    H - Homes or storefronts where the believers meet.

    The believer is now ready to join forces with you in spreading the good news of Jesus Christ.

- Return to the beginning of this training and walk through it with the new believer. Be sure to answer the four questions that he or she will have.

- Remember, new believers make the best evangelizers. All their friends are still lost, and their passion for Christ is fresh.

ENDNOTES

1 *The Purpose Driven Church*, Rick Warren (Zondervan Publishing House, Grand Rapids, 1995), p.43.

2 *Church Planting Movements*, David Garrison, pp. 312-314.

3 *Church Planting Movements*, David Garrison, pp. 315-317.

Resource Materials

Form # 1—My Family and Friends
Everyone I know who is presently unconverted

Immediate Family Members:

_____
_____
_____
_____
_____
_____

Friends:

_____
_____
_____
_____
_____
_____

Relatives:

_____
_____
_____
_____
_____
_____

Neighbors & Associates:

_____

_____

_____

_____

_____

_____

FORM # 2—MY EVANGELISTIC PRAYER LIST
The 10 people who are most open
to hearing about Jesus

Instructions: Please list below the names of the 10 people from your large name list who are the most open to hearing about Jesus at present. Please pray for them daily, asking God to give them a personal revelation of who Jesus is. Also look for opportunities to witness to them and to invite them to church or to an evangelistic crusade. Whenever one of these persons commits his life to Christ, please scratch that name out and add the name of another unsaved relative or friend.

Form # 2—My Evangelistic Prayer List
The 10 people who are most open
to hearing about Jesus

Instructions: Please list below the names of the 10 people from your large name list who are the most open to hearing about Jesus at present. Please pray for them daily, asking God to give them a personal revelation of who Jesus is. Also look for opportunities to witness to them and to invite them to church or to an evangelistic crusade. Whenever one of these persons commits his life to Christ, please scratch that name out and add the name of another unsaved relative or friend.

Form # 3
Faith Promise Commitment Form

Yes, Lord, I will make a Faith Promise to help reach my country's unreached peoples and to finish the Great Commission:

☐ By faith in God I will give _____ /month during the next year.

By claiming the financial increase from God spoken of in 2 Corinthians 9:11, I will seek to faithfully and joyfully give the above money for reaching a lost world for Jesus Christ!

Today's Date: _____

Form # 4

Instructions: Please fill out both copies of the form below. Keep one copy for yourself and post the other to: Mission Catalyst International, P. O. Box 73047, Houston, TX 77273–3047, USA. We would like to have a copy of the commitment you are making for our records.

Church Planting/UPG Commitment Form

By God's grace, I commit myself today to plant a total of at least _____ new churches among my own people-group in my country during the next 10 years. I also commit to reach a total of at least _____ un-reached people groups in my country by planting at least five strong churches among each of these groups during the next 10 years.

Name (print) _____

Signature _____

Address _____

_____

_____

_____

_____

Today's Date: _____

Name of unreached people groups that I plan to reach (if known):

1) _____

2) _____

3) _____

My people group _____

E-mail address: _____